PRIVATISING

A Study of International Privatisation
in Theory and Practice

To Richard Downer

PRIVATISING THE WORLD

A Study of International Privatisation in Theory and Practice

by
OLIVER LETWIN
International Privatisation Unit
N M Rothschild & Sons Limited

With a Foreword by
John Redwood, MP

CASSELL

Cassell Educational Ltd:
Artillery House,
Artillery Row,
London, SW1P 1RT

British Library Cataloguing in Publication Data

Letwin, Oliver
  Privatising the world : a study of
  international privatisation in theory
  and practice.
  1. Public sector. Privatisation
  I. Title
  351.007'2

ISBN 0-304-31526-5
ISBN 0-304-31527-3 Pbk

First published 1988

Typeset by Inforum Ltd, Portsmouth
Printed and bound in Great Britain by
Biddles Ltd., Guildford and Kings Lynn
Copyright © 1988 by Cassell Educational Ltd.

CONTENTS

FOREWORD

by John Redwood, MP

Privatisation is the new economic creed. It is already spawning many sects and theologies, for it represents a broad church. The idea of reducing state involvement in industry and commerce is not new. What is new is the drive to reverse the intervention of government in the economic life of many countries on a large, even heroic scale. The movement, already under way in many countries of the world, now needs a synoptic account. This book has been written as a result of the work of N.M. Rothschild in many countries of the world offering advice to governments and companies on how to be privatised. This is that account.

The spread of the privatisation movement will surprise even well-informed readers. Geographically, privatisation is taking place in most of the major Western European countries. The United Kingdom was the pioneer, setting out a large privatisation programme which could see the whole of state industry and commerce returned to the private sector within the space of some ten years. France was the next most active country to follow suit; others are now showing their hands in a similar manner. Outside Europe the process is just as widespread. In the Americas, the United States has become the leading exporter of the idea through the State Department and USAID, and at home the US administration has sold Conrail, one of its major railway companies. Canada and the Canadian provinces have embarked upon substantial programmes of privatisation. In Central and South America many countries are following the same route. Many

African territories are also treading the path of privatisation, often in an effort to reduce the debts and the losses that their state enterprises have incurred. In Asia and the Far East many countries have come to the same conclusion, often for different reasons.

As varied as the countries undertaking privatisation are the styles of privatisation they undertake. This book reveals the diversity in its full extent. The most famous type of privatisation is now that pioneered in the United Kingdom, where a major public stock market flotation is undertaken to sell control of a state-run company into private hands. But there are many other kinds of privatisation, whole or partial. Trade sales, auctions, share sales, liquidations, introducing new competitors and new investors, joint ventures between the public and private sector and franchising out activities – these are all routes that are being travelled as the world embarks on its major privatisation initiatives.

There have been many innovations to encourage the growth of stock markets and to open the way for privatisation by share sales. The privatisation process has brought to stock markets a new depth and volume. A large number of new investors have been pulled into share ownership wherever it has been tried around the world. It has turned out to be a powerful mechanism for popularising stock exchange activities and for bringing a large number of new savers into the direct ownership of industry and commerce. It has seen new techniques designed by bankers and brokers: instalment issues, where the investor makes a downpayment and then subscribes subsequent payments at future dates; tender offers where the investor writes in the price he wishes to pay and the shares are allocated at the maximum price possible; warrant issues attached to the shares which take the form of a concealed future rights issue, allowing the company to be privatised and then for the new managers to enjoy some months later the windfall of extra capital subscribed through the warrants; negotiated underwriting commissions reducing the cost to the vendor whilst at the same time guaranteeing by the underwriting that he will sell his shares whatever the market circumstances. These and many other new financial techniques have been the direct result of the pressure of privatisation upon stock markets, forcing innovation as well as the pursuit of new investors.

The origins of my interest in privatisation world-wide lay in my visit to the Washington Conference set up by USAID in February 1986. I had been actively involved as head of the Prime Minister's Policy Unit in the establishment of the much larger British privatisations after the 1983 election. I drew on my experiences as businessman and commentator on the nationalised industries during the 1970s. I was able to put to the test ideas from the books and articles I had written in the wilderness years of the 1970s urging private capital and private enterprise solutions to the problems of state industry and commerce.

On leaving Downing Street in order to take up a prospective Parliamentary candidacy in England I had to find a way of earning my living. I agreed with N.M. Rothschild that I would explore the possibilities of setting up a major non-UK privatisation business for the bank. At the Washington Conference in February 1986 were assembled the representatives of 60 nations, all interested in hearing about the theory and practice of privatisation. Several things struck me forcibly about that gathering. The first was the enthusiasm of the US administration for the idea of privatisation, despite their lack of any direct experience of it. The second was the desperation of many of the countries represented to find a way out of the predicament of being over-borrowed in a heavily indebted world where the Americans were no longer able to lend money as freely as they had in the 1970s. The third was the hesitation or the fear of many at that conference about the way in which privatisation might work in their own countries and whether indeed it was feasible at all.

I learnt enough from that conference to know that privatisation was going to become a major international phenomenon. There was a clear need for good advice from those who had direct experience of the process. People had legitimate fears. 'How could privatisation work in my country where there is no developed stock market?' 'How can it work with my government which is not right-of-centre and does not believe in the free enterprise economics of Margaret Thatcher?' 'What would the government do if it lost control of its crucial industries?' 'Would it any longer be able to have an energy policy or a defence policy?' 'Wouldn't it be better if we waited for the profits to improve or the management's performance to improve before we privatise?'

'Should we privatise a loss-making business which would be difficult to sell or a profit-making one which means we would lose the annual revenue of that corporation forever?' All these and many other questions came out at the Washington Conference and in subsequent discussions. Beneath it all it emerged that people needed not only financial guidance but also an understanding of the political dynamics of the process and of the different types of privatisation that were possible, representing different solutions to differing problems.

Oliver Letwin joined me at Rothschilds, also coming from the Prime Minister's Policy Unit. He rapidly became one of the most perceptive and knowledgeable privatisation advisers. Several governments have come to be grateful for his sage advice and enormous energy. The reader could not be in safer hands.

As the world proceeds along its course of privatisation many will claim that what had seemed improbable in 1983, what seemed difficult in 1986, was obvious all along. They are seeing the world with a misleading clarity of hindsight. It was not always obvious that privatisation would turn out to be a big multinational winner. It was only one of several techniques on offer to deal with the problems of debt, heavy loss-making public sector enterprises and economies caught in a vicious circle of low growth, high taxes, expenditure cuts and even lower growth. What people now need is a good book both to explain the techniques and to give some hard practical advice on the vested-interest politics of privatisation.

The most difficult thing of all about privatisation is that it requires a cultural shift in government itself. Governments around the world have for years been used to extending their power and their influence. Pork-barrel politics is common in rich and poor countries alike. Civil servants like their empires to grow rather than diminish. Politicians are reluctant to shed any function, however painful it may have been for them in its execution, fearing some reprisal or fearing that their colleagues will think that they lack political virility because they are surrendering part of their empire. There are always 101 reasons why a minister should not take action to get rid of that enterprise at that stage. 'Would it not, Minister, interfere at this juncture with our sensitive national policy on something or other?' 'Would it not be better, Minister, to wait until the position has improved?' 'Would it not be better to do it immediately after the next election, Minister, when the political risks will be lower?' The questions multiply the fears in the politician's mind and without firm political leadership in favour of privatisation it is better not to embark on the process.

The first advice that should always be given to governments who want to set up a privatisation programme is to establish a clear timetable. You need rules of the road which ensure that instead of decisions being deferred, put off, or continuously argued about, they have to be taken at agreed intervals. The timetable becomes the driving force behind any privatisation and everyone has to be made to believe in it. Whether or not there is the best answer available at the time at which the timetable says the decision has to be taken, the decision has to be taken. Whether or not departments want to go on bickering endlessly, with the Ministry of Finance arguing this, the Ministry of Energy arguing that, and the Prime Minister's department arguing something else, there has to be the discipline of the timetable which forces them to decide regardless of whether they are happy or not. As soon as the discipline of decision-taking is allowed to break down, the privatisation will run off the rails. There are too many vested interests between departments in all governments, too many political interests in conflict between leading politicians in all governments for it to be otherwise. It is extremely difficult in any government anywhere in the world to get something done quickly and well. The first challenge for a privatisation programme is to break that mould. To do that you need to identify a small team of ministers and civil servants who are dedicated to the process and to appoint an adviser who will be the ruthless custodian of the timetable.

Governments always wish to know whether they should go for a grand plan or a piecemeal programme. Many are attracted to the idea of the grand plan. After all, governments have for years been weened on the notion that planning of all kinds is but an extension of general economic planning, so go for a plan of general privatisation. It also defers the evil day when anything has to be resolved. You can spend six months asking the question whether to have a grand plan or not with one set of consultants. Then you can spend another six months to a year with another set of consultants advising you on the grand plan. You can then spend six months to a year in having a delightful political fight over the implications of the grand plan. Is it grand enough, or is it too grand? Are the asset sales in the right order? Have people thought about absolutely everything that could go wrong? What if the stock market could not stand it? What if the new investors did not emerge? The questions can multiply endlessly.

There are examples world-wide of successful grand plans and unsuccessful ones. The French showed that it can be done if you have the will to do it swiftly and well. They confined their grand plan to an enabling statute which gave them all the powers they needed to sell assets without going back each time to the parliament. It caused a short, sharp political row but it was one well worth having. They are now in a very strong position to have a fast and impressive privatisation programme. In contrast, several countries have shown how easy it is to spend a large amount of money on consultancy advice without ever getting anywhere. They put thinking and planning before doing. As a result, some countries that once looked as though they would have important privatisation programmes are still trying to get around to their first major privatisation.

Each country has to work out its own methods. If the politicians have sufficient courage to grasp a grand plan and to discipline it then by all means do it, especially if enabling legislation can be taken to reduce the individual political hassle over each subsequent privatisation. But it is only for the brave and the strong. Otherwise the piecemeal approach is much better. For a grand plan can also produce a grand coalition of vested interests against privatisation and give Civil Service opposition the time to build up to block it. Privatisation has to be carried out quickly and momentum will build up of its own accord. It is not until politicians discover that privatisation can be successful and can enhance their own careers that the tide turns in any administration.

The next question that arises is what kind of privatisation the country should undertake. As this book shows, there are many types. The prior question which a country has to ask is what are the aims of the privatisation programme it has in mind. As this book also shows, there can be many such aims.

So a government embarking on a privatisation policy has first of all to settle in its own mind what it wants to do and why it wishes to do it. There may be an amalgam of motives. It is quite possible for a government to want to widen share ownership in its country, to allow employees to obtain a stake in the businesses for which they work, to wish to see an improvement in the performance of the management of national assets and to raise money at the same time. In many of the largest and most successful privatisation programmes all these aims and others are present. But in each particular privatisation, it is important to ask what the prior aim is. Otherwise it is too easy to fall between all the stools and to get unsatisfactory results.

There are many worries which governments have when embarking on a privatisation policy. The first and most obvious one is that they might lose policy control. Governments have got used to running oil industries, electricity industries, transport industries and the like. What might happen, they ask, to our bus services if we no longer have the ability to choose to run a bus service along this route or if we no longer have the right to subsidise the fares? What might happen to our oil reserves if we allow the private sector to exploit them without controls? Could we be left in a crisis without oil supplies? What might happen to our regional policy, to employment opportunities within our large public industries and indeed what might happen to the defence of our country if crucial manufacturing enterprises were given over to private control?

These are easy difficulties to resolve if politicians wish to resolve them. In many ways it is easier to control an industry which you do not own than one which you do. As soon as you own it and are answerable for its financial results all kinds of compromises have to be made and accommodations reached. None of the underlying policy issues which are thought to be raised by nationalised industries relate to whether or not the industries are nationalised. It is quite possible to have a sane energy policy which does lay down what happens in a crisis of supply or what the rules are about trading oil or gas produced within your country without owning all the assets concerned. It is quite possible to subsidise bus or rail fares without owning the tracks or the buses.

In many ways it is simplier to settle on the level of public subsidy by allowing tenders from those who wish to run the services. You then have the added ability to sack the tenderer or terminate his agreement if the service is unsatisfactory. This is a luxury you rarely enjoy when you own the business itself, as governments are bad at removing managements that have failed and have nowhere else to go when they own the complete monopoly business.

Another set of worries relates to what the markets can stand: if the government is getting financial advice that the stock markets of the countries concerned will not allow the programme to be undertaken, it should change its financial advisers. Traditional prudent financial advisers have given this advice all around the world and they have been systematically wrong. The capacity of the French market doubled in the first year of major privatisations. The capacity of the London equity market has multiplied tenfold over the decade of privatisation, partly as a result of the magnitude of the privatisation equity issues. The Jamaican Stock Market showed itself capable of expanding dramatically to undertake two major privatisations in 18 months.

The World Stock Market crash of October 1987 which damaged the UK government's BP issue, served to remind the world of the risks of equity investment and the dangers of buying stock in an overvalued market. It does not sound the death knell of the march into private equity: it merely means the next major issue will have to be attractively priced. There is an inevitability about the growth of capital markets, because the world is overborrowed and needs more capital.

It requires some planning to expand a stock market. But above all it requires equity issues to increase capacity. Dealing capacity will usually expand to carry out the deals available. Financial capacity will increase as the economy becomes more prosperous and as the stock market grows. One of the major points of privatisation is to increase the number of domestic savers who wish to use the stock market to invest their moneys. A successful programme in a developing country can succeed in encouraging people to keep their money in the country concerned rather than furtively sending it outside the country, breaking the usual exchange control rules.

Governments will then have to contend with the favourite

delaying tactic, the doctrine of the unripe time. Those who wish to stop privatisation will, beyond a certain point, accept that they have lost the argument of principle. They will shift their ground to saying that it will be better to leave it for a year or two. Governments have to remember that the time is never entirely ripe to do anything. But they should also remember that there is a great risk in doing nothing. If you carry on running a nationalised industry which is profitable you may find that next year something has gone wrong, it has lost money and is another headache. If you are running a nationalised industry that is not profitable or unpopular why carry on bashing your head against a brick wall when there may be a better way of having it managed by someone else? The best advice to governments facing the trial of the unripe time is to use other civil servants to get the policy through as quickly as possible.

The newest problem to emerge in privatisation is the problem of monopoly. In the United Kingdom the privatisation pro-gramme has expanded so rapidly that it now encompasses the sale of major state public utility monopolies. British Telecom and British Gas have already been sold to the public and there has been an active debate about how to sell the biggest of them all, the electricity industry. Without careful handling, the problem of monopoly can bring privatisation into disrepute. It is one of those curious facts of political life that because the monopoly has been nationalised for many years people get used to a poor-quality service, lack of choice, and often to successive large price in-creases. They begin to believe the rhetoric that because it is publicly owned, somehow everything will be all right. They believe that although there is every evidence to see that public ownership has not succeeded in the past in taming a monopoly, it would be far worse if that monopoly were to be put into the private sector.

There is one reason why these fears should be taken seriously. A monopoly transferred to the private sector without controls could easily fall into the hands of those who not only wish to perpetuate bad service and high prices but also to exploit the pricing power the monopoly enjoys to make even bigger profits. There is a danger that the private monopolist will close certain types of service that are unprofitable which the public utility, through sloth or generosity of spirit, has carried on running. There is an even bigger probability that a privatised monopoly will be even harsher on prices unless it is controlled.

But the act of privatisation enables the government to change the rules. Why should governments go on owning large public monopolies that often perform badly, leaving themselves with all the criticism of the standard of service every time the prices go up? There is a much better alternative on offer.

The best option of all is to open the monopoly up to competition. In the case of British Telecom this is exactly what has happened. The criticisms of the British Telecom privatisation centre around those areas of the business which were not opened up to competition quickly enough or at all. Where competition was introduced, as in the provision of telephone equipment to the end-user and in the supply of value added network services there has been practically no criticism and a great deal of improvement in the quality and range of services on offer. British Telecom's market share of end-user equipment has fallen every year since this area was de-monopolised. There has been a large increase in the range and quality of products on offer.

It would have been possible to go even faster in introducing alternative network providers. In the United Kingdom it was decided to license only one alternative network, Mercury. The interesting question will arise in 1990 when the government has to decide whether the time has come to produce yet more competitors. I hope it will decide that it is vital to do so. For only if there is genuine competition across all sections of the network can the government satisfactorily answer the criticism that elements of private monopoly remain and the service is inadequate.

If a government wishes to sell a monopoly but remains cautious of introducing competition it does have a less satisfactory option as well. It is probably the case that a properly regulated private monopoly is preferable to an unregulated public one.

In the case of British Telecom the imposition of a single but strict price control has produced a much better deal for the customer on prices since privatisation than the customer ever enjoyed under the nationalised industry. The problem with regulation when it comes to service quality and the range of service provisions is that it has to become quite detailed, but the more detailed it becomes the more of the other benefits of privatisation in terms of management freedom and innovation are likely to be lost. There has to be a trade-off in formulating the regulations. The detailed thrust the government feels it needs to guarantee customer rights and to protect itself against obvious political criticisms on the one hand, has to be reconciled with the need to avoid too detailed a series of regulations that can quickly become dated and can in themselves become an obstacle to sensible management on the other.

It is important in the United Kingdom that when electricity comes to be privatised competition will be given its full head. People always argue that things that happen to be national public monopolies are natural monopolies and that therefore the pursuit of competition is the pursuit of the will-o'-the-wisp. This is usually untrue. In the case of electricity, 80 per cent of the cost of electricity to the end-user is the cost of the fuel burnt and the capital cost of the power station generating the electricity. There is no element of natural monopoly whatsoever in the generation of power for a medium-sized or large country. Generating sets usually have a capacity of around 1,000 megawatts. These are the relevant unit of account. It is possible to have a diversified ownership structure for the generation of electricity in all but the smallest of countries. The British government White Paper proposals of February 1988 recognise this and recommend introducing several competitors into generation. Once you have diversity and competition in generation you have a market test on the costs of capital construction, the financing of the plant, efficiencies of the plant and on the fuel choice and buying practices. It has been this absence of competitive pressure on all these costs that has led to so many problems in electricity industries around the world.

Similarly, in the oil and gas industries people sometimes suggest that there has to be a natural national monopoly protected by statute. Yet the unit of account for the production of gas and oil is the oilfield or gasfield itself. Private sector exploitation shows that this can be achieved with diversified ownership of units as small as a single oilfield.

In the transport industries, road surface transport is never a natural monopoly. In the case of buses or lorries, the individual capital unit is small and the optimum size of the organisational unit may be quite modest in scale. No one has demonstrated greatly superior performance from widespread economies of scale that might theoretically be achieved by having a national monopoly system. In the case of the railways, where there is a large fixed-way infrastructure, those who argue the natural monopoly case do have slightly better grounds. However, there is no reason why the provision of ancillary services on stations, catering, or even the running of trains themselves over the permanent fixed way need be a monopoly. There is every reason to suppose that competitive tendering to run trains and use station facilities would generate more revenue and more customer satisfaction.

To all governments thinking of privatisation, the evidence of the British experience must be that you have to be careful when privatising monopolies. People should not be forced to conclude, however, that there are a lot of natural monopolies or that these can never be privatised. The evidence of the British experience is that the policy can work very well and be very popular if and when sufficient competition is introduced. Indeed some of the most important advances world-wide in encouraging economic growth and improved micro-economic efficiency are likely to come from the widespread adoption of deregulatory policies towards the telecommunications industries in a variety of countries. Once the old public utility monopolies are swept away a large increase in value added network services and other types of service using telecommunications equipment takes place quite quickly. Telecommunications infrastructure is now probably the most forceful of all the capital provision needed to foster rapid growth for an advanced society. It may well be that, when the history books come to be written, the deregulation of telecommunications industries turns out to be the most significant point of all in the widespread deregulation and privatisation movement worldwide.

Privatisation is a policy for all seasons and for many reasons. It can bring many benefits to the government undertaking it. It can bring a bigger and more sophisticated stock market, which in its turn can expedite the financing of private industry. It can bring better company results and more enterprise in areas of the economy that have been ossified by public monopoly ownership. It can bring a better spirit between managers and employees and can produce a unifying political theme under the banner of wider ownership. It can, above all, produce money for the government to spend on other desired social programmes or begin to cut the horrendous levels of borrowing that so many governments burdened themselves with in the 1960s and 1970s.

In order to be successful governments need a good adviser dedicated to the success of their privatisation programmes and sensitive to the government's political situation. The adviser should be the custodian of a vigorous timetable to drive through the necessary decisions, and equipped with good political antennae, for the whole process is about politics as much as it is about finance. This book illustrates the collective wisdom of a group of people who have worked hard on privatisation in a wide variety of conditions. Its range and its scope equip it well to be the first bible of this new world-wide economic religion. Read it well and you will find, whether you are a businessman, politician or civil servant, that the world is never quite the same again.

1

PRIVATISATION: ITS ORIGINS AND EXTENT

The Nationalised Industries

The origins of state ownership and state-run services are lost in the mists of time. For as long as there have been rulers, they have owned lands and buildings and have provided food and clothing for retainers. With the gradual emergence of more abstract concepts such as the Crown and the state, those assets and services previously owned or carried out by the ruler began to be controlled by departments of state and servants of the Crown, and – through commands and franchises – local authorities were entrusted with items of common interest such as roads, ports and bridges, thereby establishing the concept of specifically 'public' activities.

The origins of the 'private' sector are even more deeply buried. Whether primitive trade was carried on by individuals within our ancestoral tribes, or only collectively on behalf of the tribe as a whole, is a matter for endless speculation. But private enterprise of many sorts – in manufacturing, trading and services – was certainly a feature of ancient civilisations. Indeed, in ancient Rome, the level of private enterprise was sufficient to stir eloquent complaints from Horace and other puritanical commentators. Crassus, perhaps the richest and most ruthlessly enterprising of all the Romans, is reputed to have run an interesting combination of a private property firm and a private fire service, with what would now be described as a synergy between the two: buying houses at a low price when burning and then sending the fire-engines speedily to rescue his new-found property.

1

Even if control of the land, and hence of agriculture, was in the hands of the sovereign during the feudal era, private enterprise nevertheless flourished in the towns, where craftsmen, weavers and traders abounded, and where the market was the centre of all activity. Gradually, a plethora of private professionals and service-providers came into being, springing either from private initiative (as in the case of the bankers) or from the Church and other public institutions (as in the case of the lawyers). In Britain during the sixteenth and seventeenth centuries, and in other countries at various times, clearly recognisable 'private sector' joint-stock companies also began to emerge: the Russia Company appears to have been the first example, founded in 1553. Joint-stock arrangements gradually became a common method of funding voyages; by 1600, the East India Company had begun and investments in it, which had originally been only for a single voyage, became permanent in the second half of the seventeenth century, yielding a company in the modern sense. Meanwhile, the Bank of England was established as a private sector joint-stock company issuing loan stock on behalf of the government, and brokers both in the equity of the joint-stock companies and in government loan stock began trading actively in the early eighteenth century. By 1773, London had an official stock exchange. With the coming of the canals and the railways the volume of private capitalism grew tremendously, and by the time of the Companies Act 1862 the modern concept of a private sector limited liability company was firmly established.

Economies have, in other words, been 'mixed' since time out of mind. The 'public sector' and the 'private sector', in many different and often hazily distinguished forms, have been present together throughout history. It is therefore impossible to say, and senseless to ask, when the first 'nationalised industry' or 'state-run service' was set up. Nor is it by any means clear what one should define as nationalisation and what should be called a traditional activity of government. In Australia, Austria, Belgium, Brazil, Britain, Canada, France, West Germany, India, Italy, Japan, South Korea, Mexico, the Netherlands, Singapore, Spain, Sweden, Switzerland, the USA, and no doubt dozens of other countries, governments set up post offices at some time or other as Departments of State. Were these intrinsically 'nationalised

2

industries', despite being departments rather than corporations? And if so, by what criteria are they to be distinguished from national armies and municipal fire services? In many countries – particularly the young countries of North America, Australasia and the Third World – most of the activities which would commonly be called nationalised industries were created in this way: a department of state set up a new function or service in an effort to establish efficient utilities or effective communications because, for one reason or another, the private sector had not yet done so. In such cases, it is misleading even to talk of 'nationalisation' when describing the growth of the public sector.

In Britain, however, and in some other countries, particularly in Europe, 'nationalisation' is a distinct phenomenon. True, the British post office (and later its telephone branch), some of the public sector ports, and the BBC were set up as state enterprises from the start, either as departments of the government or corporations owned by the state. But between 1946 and 1949 the British government made a conscious effort to nationalise industries which had previously been in private hands. Clause 4 of the Labour Party Constitution stated that the Party existed 'to secure for the producers by hand and brain the full fruits of their industry, and the most equitable distribution thereof that may be possible on the basis of the common ownership of the means of production'. Guided by this doctrine, the Labour government of the late 1940s took into public ownership the Bank of England, the coal industry, the major airlines, railways, road haulage, gas, iron and steel, and electricity. In the 1970s, the government added to the national portfolio shares in other transport companies, as well as Rolls-Royce, British Leyland, British Aerospace, British Shipbuilders and a multitude of holdings in high-technology companies, such as Ferranti, Cable and Wireless, and Amersham International.

In France, too, there were large-scale nationalisations. During the late 1930s, munitions factories and aircraft manufacturers were nationalised. Then, between 1944 and 1947, a major programme began, nationalising electricity, coal, gas, Renault cars, the Bank of France, and other banks and insurance companies. The state subsequently acquired major share-holdings in rail, petroleum, chemicals, construction, airlines and communications, with a final burst of nationalisation in 1981–2 transferring some 700,000 jobs to the public sector.

By the late 1970s, a combination of the establishment of new industries or specific services by the state and the nationalisation of companies previously existing in the private sector had vastly increased the size of the public sector in most of the Western world. Differing definitions of 'public' and gaps in other economic data make global comparisons and precise figures difficult to construct; but one reputable estimate published by the IMF in 1984 suggests that, in the years 1974–7, public enterprise (excluding public sector holdings in financial corporations) accounted for an average of 13.4 per cent of total investment in 77 mixed economies, and for an average of 16.5 per cent of total investment if the United States is excluded (Henry Parris, Pierre Pestieau and Peter Saynor, *Public Enterprise in Western Europe*, Croom Helm, London, 1987). The proportion of investment occupied by the public sector in developing countries over the same period seems to have been even higher, reaching 20 per cent – a figure paralleled in some European countries, such as Austria and the UK. Moreover, these figures greatly understate the significance of the public sector in certain areas of the economy. In the early 1980s, public enterprises accounted for close to 50 per cent of the total fixed investment in all enterprises employing 20 or more people in both France and Italy; though such enterprises interestingly accounted only for about 25 per cent of total employees and gross domestic product, indicating the heavy bias of the public sector towards capital-intensive industry. In some specific industries, the dominance of the state at the end of the 1970s was even greater: in a large number of countries, over 75 per cent of telecommunications, electricity, gas, coal, railways and airlines were in the public sector, and in some cases a similar proportion of oil production, the motor industry, the steel industry, the shipbuilding industry and the aerospace industry were in the government's hands.

The size of the undertakings implied by these figures is staggering. The Ministry of Finance in Japan estimated that, in 1975, approximately 900,000 people were employed in public corporations; the nationalised industries in Italy employed some 1.3 million people in 1981–2; 1.6 million people were employed

4

in nationalised industries in the UK in the same year, and some 2.4. million were employed in some 500 French public enterprises in 1982. At their largest, many of the nationalised industries were individually enormous: Nippon Telegraph and Telephone employed some 308,000 employees in 1975; Japan National Railways employed over 430,000 in the same year; and in 1953 the National Coal Board in the UK had 707,000 employees, making it larger than the entire present British Civil Service.

These large capital-intensive trading corporations were, however, only a small part of the picture. Increasingly, since the beginning of the twentieth century, it is public services rather than public corporations that have come to dominate public sector employment figures. In the UK, at its height, the locally provided education service alone employed well over 500,000 people, with hundreds of thousands more in other local services and the National Health Service. Local public enterprises in Japan, of which there were some 7,000 in 1975, employed over 300,000 people. And the total number of employees in the municipal services in the USA almost certainly dwarfs any other single form of economic activity in the world.

The Pre-History of Privatisation

The performance and public perception of nationalised industries and public services have been different in different cases and countries. In the USA, where the extent of nationalisation at the federal level has always been extremely limited, and in Canada (where most of the 'Crown corporations' were set up from scratch rather than being private companies taken over by the state), there is relatively little sign of popular discontent with the performance of nationalised industries. This is partly because of the high levels of service and low prices which the US and Canadian examples have provided for the customer: Amtrak, in the United States, provides fast, reliable passenger rail travel at low cost, while the Canadian provincial hydro-electric companies have generally provided continuous, low-cost electricity supplies to domestic and industrial users even in outlying communities. Whether these

5

operations are economically efficient is altogether another matter, but customers have been satisfied with them.

In some other countries, such as Turkey, Mexico and Italy, the nationalised industries, though often extremely inefficient, have been regarded more or less as a way of life. They have been maintained by successive governments of differing political complexions and have employed large numbers of people with apparent popular acquiescence. Their reputation has in many cases been poor, but this does not appear to have generated any noticeable political stirrings against their existence until the 1980s.

In the UK, the history is somewhat different. For various reasons, including a very poor industrial relations record, peculiarly uncommercial attitudes and apparently insufficient concern for the interests of the customer, nationalised industries became exceedingly unpopular. As early as January 1951, a public opinion poll found that only 24 per cent of the population approved of the nationalisation of iron and steel, while 54 per cent disapproved (R. Eatwell, *The 1945–1951 Labour Governments*, Batsford Academic Press, London, 1979). Repeated opinion polls over the following 30 years continued to show that nationalisation and the nationalised industries were highly unpopular. One survey carried out by National Opinion Polls in 1982 showed that over 60 per cent of those interviewed opposed further nationalisation and believed that nationalised industries were less efficient than private sector companies, while only 16 per cent wanted further nationalisation and only 12 per cent believed that nationalised industries were on the whole more efficient. As a result, politicians displayed continuing concern, establishing a Parliamentary Select Committee on Nationalised Industries, which conducted 39 separate scrutinies between October 1957 and July 1978. Governments responded with a series of White Papers, in which they attempted to tighten the financial screws and to ensure that the industries produced reasonable rates of return on capital employed. Despite these investigations and efforts, however, many of the nationalised industries remained unprofitable, strike-ridden and inefficient from the consumer's point of view. In 1978–9, the British Steel Corporation – perhaps the most lurid example – lost one-sixth of its capital in a single trading year. In

6

the same year, British Leyland was operating with machinery roughly twice as old as that of its major competitors, and the nationalised industries as a whole were absorbing some £2.5 billion (in 1978–9 terms) of taxpayer's money.

Perhaps because of the particularly low esteem in which the British nationalised industries were held, Conservative governments in Britain made frequent attempts to denationalise. In 1953, the Transport Act denationalised road haulage; in 1960, the Civil Aviation (Licensing) Act ended the monopoly of the nationalised airlines. In 1966, Edward Heath proclaimed at the Party Conference that 'the Conservative Party is the Party of free enterprise', while the 1966 Conservative Party *Campaign Guide* quoted a former Civil Servant as saying that 'in fact, the State can exercise a more flexible and powerful control over an industry by *not* owning it'. Between 1971 and 1973, the Heath government hived off BOAC routes to the private British Caledonian, sold the Thomas Cook travel agency, and denationalised the Carlisle state breweries.

These denationalisations are, however, no more than the pre-history of privatisation. They did not amount to a coherent programme: indeed, Conservative governments in the UK over the same period were responsible for setting up new nationalised industries such as the BBC, the Central Electricity Generating Board, and the Atomic Energy Authority, as well as for nationalising coal royalties and for taking Rolls-Royce into public ownership when the company went bankrupt. Moreover, the policy, in so far as it was a policy at all, was almost entirely negative: it consisted of undoing a nationalisation which had been brought about by some previous government, without any idea that the fundamental relationship between the state and the industry or the underlying nature of the economy would be altered by a positive programme of privatisation. As a result, these early denationalisations were relatively small in scale, had little popular appeal, and were easily reversible. A classic example is the British iron and steel industry, which was first nationalised in 1951 (following the Iron and Steel Act 1949), was denationalised again in slow stages between 1953 and 1963 (with some steel firms remaining under national ownership even then), and renationalised in 1967.

In most other countries, such early privatisation as occurred followed the same, rather incoherent and indecisive pattern. For example, the conservatively inclined Norwegian government in 1965 (coming to power after a socialist government which had nationalised post, telephone, rail, power, mining, alcoholic drinks, medical supplies and other industrial and commercial sectors) engaged in a small-scale denationalisation programme, selling off such items as a fish-processing factory and some mining and aluminium plants – hardly sufficient to create a new political or economic landscape. In Canada, the Clark administration of the late 1970s also adopted a privatisation programme, and announced a willingness to sell five major firms, including Petro-Canada. But little actually happened. Petro-Canada, instead of being sold, was merely prevented from expanding further into areas occupied by the private sector, and other major candidates for sale (including De Havilland and Teleglobe) remained in state hands – ready for another Conservative government in the 1980s to reconsider.

In West Germany, more imaginative ideas were applied. The government in 1959 arranged what was probably the first 'modern' public privatisation offer, with the sale of a block of shares in Preussag (an electricity and mining company) to the public; foreshadowing later developments in the UK, there were special concessions for employees and small shareholders who participated in the offer. This was followed by a public offer of shares in Volkswagen – a privatisation which attracted 1.5 million shareholders. In 1965 and 1966, there were further sales of government stakes in the heavy industrial and communications conglomerate, VEBA, and in Lufthansa. But these moves – though adventurous in conception and significant in scale – never developed into a coherent political and economic programme capable of catching the popular imagination.

In British Columbia, an even more adventurous attempt was made. The government of the aptly named Social Credit Party, under the leadership of W.A.C. Bennett, brought together a series of public sector investments, including shares in a cellulose company, two forest-products companies, and a natural gas company, into a single holding company named the British Columbia Resources Investment Corporation. In January 1979,

8

it was announced that each inhabitant of British Columbia would receive five free shares in the new corporation, and that each would also be entitled to buy up to 5,000 shares. An elaborate system of checks was devised to determine whether individual applicants were eligible. Applications began in March 1979; by July 1979 some 2 million people (or 86 per cent of the eligible population) had applied for the free shares and almost C$500 million had been raised from the accompanying sale. This brave experiment was not, however, followed by further sales, and never developed into a fully fledged privatisation programme. As BCRIC shares climbed in value, and then began to drop (probably due to weak management), the public – who displayed increasing enthusiasm in the early years – began to show signs of disenchantment, and the whole episode is now regarded as at best a mixed success.

The Rise of Liberal Economic Policies in the UK

In the 1970s, British Conservatives began to sketch out a more coherent programme of privatisation. One central figure, Rhodes Boyson (later a minister in the Thatcher government) edited a book entitled *Goodbye to Nationalisation* (Churchill Press, London, 1971). If this title did not speak for itself, an even more explicit subtitle was provided: 'A Symposium on the Failure of the "Publicly" Controlled Industries and the Need to Return Them to a Competitive Framework'. In his introductory essay to the volume, Boyson was equally explicit:

> The need to break up and sell off the nationalised industries must be part of a new free enterprise way of life ... share ownership and control of industry must be spread as widely as possible ... between 1951 to 1954 the Conservative Governments were content to denationalise steel and long-distance road haulage. 'Disengagement' this time must go much further. The Volkswagen denationalisation ... should be a pattern to follow in mainstream industry, while all ancillary activities are sold off by public auction to the highest bidder.

General opinion in the British Conservative Party took some while to catch up with this change in mood. The official *Campaign*

9

Guide of 1970 stated that Conservatives 'oppose nationalisation, both as the ultimate extreme in state control and because accumulated practical experience has fully justified Conservative fears'; but the document went on to stress that 'the Conservative presumption in favour of free enterprise does not imply a dogmatic approach . . . Conservatives fully recognise that in a modern economy the government inevitably exerts strong influence in the affairs of industry; that special circumstances may often justify state help or intervention'. In 1972, Christopher Chataway (at that time a minister in Heath's government), wrote in a pamphlet produced by the Conservative Political Centre that 'the brave hopes of earlier generations of socialists have been washed away by post-war history. We have seen the grim, grave brutality of life in countries where the means of production, distribution and exchange *are* nationalised', but carefully added that 'there are occasions, such as occurred with Rolls-Royce, where for defence or other reasons . . . there is no short run alternative', and took the view that nationalisation was suitable for 'a few basic monopolies' and was 'a temporary expedient or a last resort' in other cases (C. Chataway, *New Deal for Industry*, Conservative Political Centre, London, 1972).

The moment when the Conservative Party officially changed its mind is difficult to date, but it is probably to be found at the end of 1976 or the beginning of 1977, soon after Mrs Thatcher became leader. The difference is brought out in two documents, both of which were official party publications. *The Right Approach*, produced in 1976, stated rather lamely: 'In some cases it may also be appropriate to sell back to private enterprise assets or activities where willing buyers can be found.' By 1977, a new document, *The Right Approach to the Economy*, stated much more stridently: 'The long-term aim must be to reduce the preponderance of state ownership and widen the base of ownership in our community. Ownership by the state is not the same as ownership by the people.' Meanwhile, Mrs Thatcher and Sir Keith Joseph were sponsoring an independent Centre for Policy Studies, which was taking an even stronger line than the party publications. In a 1975 pamphlet entitled, *Why Britain Needs a Social Market Economy*, the new Centre took the view that: 'There is now abundant evidence that state enterprises in the UK have not served well either their

10

customers, or their employees, or the tax payers. For when the state owns, nobody owns; and when nobody owns, nobody cares.' This was matched by independent commentators such as John Redwood, who set out a programme for a major rolling back of the state in *Public Enterprise in Crisis* (Blackwell, Oxford, 1980). Between the late 1970s and the mid-1980s, the new view became firmly established as official policy, and was being openly promoted by those most closely associated with the government. By 1986, John Moore, MP, then the minister specifically responsible for privatisation, was writing in a pamphlet for the Conservative Political Centre that:

The momentum is very strong and the process irreversible. . . . Possession means power, the kind of power that matters to ordinary people – power to make choices, power to control their own lives. Our aim is to extend this power to as many people as we can. We are doing it by extending ownership as widely as possible. We are doing this because we believe it is the best, indeed the only way to achieve the prosperity we seek and to protect the freedoms we value (J. Moore, *The Value of Ownership*, Conservative Political Centre, London, 1986).

During the same year, Ferdinand Mount (formerly head of the Prime Minister's Policy Unit), writing in another Conservative Political Centre pamphlet, went even further:

The greatest single reform of the machinery of government is for government to leave undone those things which ought not to be done. If this government has succeeded in its aim of halving the size of the state sector by the time of the next election, it will have done more to make us better governed than any other government in living memory (F. Mount, *The Practice of Liberty*, Conservative Political Centre, London, 1986).

Applying the New Policies

In the first two years of the Thatcher government, little was done to implement these new ideas. The main activity was, surprisingly, in municipal and local services, with the beginnings of the privatisation of council houses, as individual tenants were given the right to buy, and the gradual contracting-out of local authority services such as street cleaning and refuse collection. Some elements of deregulation and private sector competition in areas previously dominated by nationalised industries were also introduced – with, for example, the creation of competition in the provision of telephone head sets. But the only major public divestment of shares in a nationalised industry during the first two years of the new government was the sale of 5 per cent of British Petroleum, reducing the government's stake to 46 per cent, and hence officially returning the company to the private sector. Apart from this, the only privatisations of central government holdings were the privately negotiated sales of two subsidiaries of the British Technology Group: the engineering company, Fairey, was sold to a Pearson subsidiary in June 1980, and the British Technology Group's remaining holding in Ferranti was placed with institutional investors in July 1980.

The programme began to gather momentum in 1981 with the sales of British Aerospace and Cable and Wireless, closely followed in 1982 and 1983 by the sales of Amersham International, the National Freight Corporation, Britoil and Associated British Ports. Throughout the early months of 1984 (in the second term of Mrs Thatcher's government) the pressure increased, with private sales of Sealink, Inmos and the Wytch Farm assets of British Gas, and with public issues of Enterprise Oil and Jaguar.

The watershed, of course, establishing British privatisation as a major new phenomenon, was the sale of British Telecom in November 1984. Some 2.3 million individuals bought shares, with gross proceeds from the sale approaching £4 billion; sales in major markets across the world made the international headlines. Since the British Telecom sale, privatisations have been coming thick and fast. At the local level, over 1 million council houses have now been sold, and the government is introducing ambitious new plans to extend this privatisation through the creation of tenant co-operatives; new measures to enforce competitive tendering and hence to encourage contracting-out of local services are being introduced; 14 private sales of central government

12

assets have been arranged; major public issues of British Gas, British Airways, Rolls-Royce and British Airports Authority have all been completed and the remaining government share in British Petroleum has been sold. The Conservative manifesto of 1987 promised to 'continue the successful programme', to 're-turn to the public the water authorities', and to 'bring forward proposals for privatising the electricity industry'.

The scale of the programme is impressive. The gross proceeds of the sales so far conducted exceed £24 billion. And it looks as if the future will bring even larger sales, with the water boards and electricity supply industry alone accounting for another £25 billion or more of gross proceeds. Partly because of its scale, the British experience has attracted a large amount of international attention. With the continuing political success of the Thatcher government, now re-elected for the third time, privatisation has come to be seen as a politically attractive option. At international conferences held on privatisation – now almost a monthly event – the British programme is discussed in detail, and its political advantages are extolled. In France, too, privatisation is frequently cited as the government's major success story. Privatisation and success are increasingly identified with one another.

A particular testimony to the extent of this success is the change in the British Labour Party's attitude towards privatisa-tion. In an official Party document, *Labour's Programme*, pub-lished in 1982, the Party stated that:

> We believe it is wrong that private individuals should, through ownership of the means of production, reap the benefits of the collective effort of others and exercise unaccountable power over the lives of ordinary people . . . an extension of common ownership is essential in order to underpin our plan for growth and to help set new standards of public accountability and industrial democracy.

In Labour's manifesto of 1983, this point was made even more explicit:

> We will . . . return to public ownership the public assets and rights hived off by the Tories, with compensation of no more

13

than that received when the assets were denationalised. We will establish a significant public stake in electronics, pharmaceuticals, health equipment and building materials; and also in other important assets, as required by the national interest.

Between 1983 and 1987, as the scale and pace of the privatisation programme increased, the Labour Party gradually abandoned this sort of rhetoric. Instead of outright renationalisation, the Party's manifesto of 1987 talked of 'social ownership' and stated that:

We shall start by using the existing 49 per cent holding in British Telecom to ensure influence in their decisions. Private shares in B.T. and British Gas will be converted into special new securities. These will be bought and sold in the market in the usual way and will carry either a guaranteed return, or dividends linked to the company's growth.

Observing this switch of policy on the left, commentators abroad have concluded that the British privatisation programme has, indeed, special political qualities. The sale of British Gas, for example, caught the attention of the press in the USA. Even the sedate *Wall Street Journal* reported that the privatisation could serve a political purpose, increasing the number of shareholders and making voters fear a Labour government. The *Christian Science Monitor* (3 December 1986) became more excited, latching onto the advertising campaign for British Gas:

Sid, probably the most popular, most elusive person in Britain today, is British Gas's gimmick to arouse widespread public interest in buying British Gas shares. Telling Sid has become something of a national pastime. Other commercial organisations are telling Sid he'd be better off putting his money elsewhere. Truck drivers who don't take care to wash the layers of winter grime off their vehicles see written in the grime: 'This truck needs washing. Tell Sid.'

The Spread of Privatisation:
Other Governments of the Right

From the early 1980s, the leaders of the right in France began to take an increasing interest in the British programme. A formal proposition favouring privatisation in France was put forward in the Senate in May 1982. Chirac, Barre and Giscard d'Estaing all made statements in favour of privatisation. An opinion poll conducted in April 1985 showed that 44 per cent favoured privatisation of the banks, with 27 per cent opposing, and that 36 per cent favoured privatisation of other nationalised industries apart from Renault, the postal service and telecommunications, as against 26 per cent opposing. Four separate studies, describing how privatisation could be achieved, were conducted by political ginger groups, in addition to two major works written by independent experts. Senior advisers visited Britain to talk to merchant banks and Treasury officials. In short, a general atmosphere of enthusiasm was created.

When France's Conservative–Liberal coalition came to power in March 1986 it was no surprise to see privatisation as one of its commitments. Specifically, the government promised to reverse the nationalisation programme carried out in 1981–2 by the previous Socialist–Communist alliance government and to privatise the clearing banks and insurance companies brought into the public sector in 1945–6. Initially, there were difficulties because of the apparent unwillingness of the Socialist President Mitterrand to approve privatisation; and a somewhat elaborate chain of command was established with what appeared to be a degree of friction between M. Balladur, the Minister of Finance, and the subordinate minister directly responsible for privatisation, M. Cabana. These initial difficulties were, however, rapidly overcome. Cabana disappeared from the scene, leaving Balladur firmly in charge of the process, and an impressive general law permitting privatisation was promulgated in July 1986. This law is an entirely French invention without precedent in the UK or elsewhere, and has proved to be an extremely effective weapon. In principle, it is extremely simple. Article IV states merely that:

The majority holdings of the state in the enterprises listed in

15

the annex to this law will be transferred from the public sector to the private sector before 1 March 1991. These transfers will be carried out by the government in conformity with rules laid out in ordinances under article V.

The annex listed 65 companies that were to be privatised and a further law of 6 August 1986 laid out precisely the form these privatisations were to take. In particular:

1. An independent commission was to be established, and was to be charged with the duty of setting a minimum price for the sale of any state asset.
2. Sales were to be allowed either through the financial market or through private placement.
3. Special provisions were made for accepting gilts and *certificats d'investissements* in exchange for shares.
4. The Finance Minister was given specific powers to limit an individual owner's share in any given company to 5 per cent.
5. Foreign share holdings in privatised companies were limited to 20 per cent and provisions for a 'special share' were made to entrench this where necessary.
6. Employees were given special rights, including the right to have their demands for shares satisfied up to 10 per cent of the total share offering, and a right to receive a discount of up to 20 per cent (with a duty to retain shares for two years) or up to 5 per cent (with no duty to retain shares). A limit of three years was set for employees to pay for shares.
7. Special provisions were made to ensure that those applying for small numbers of shares (below ten) would be fully satisfied, and provisions were made for the issue of bonus shares to small investors (though these provisions have not always proved possible to apply in practice).

The effect of these laws was to permit rapid privatisation on a large scale without further need to consult the legislature – a programme which was feasible not only because the laws themselves were skilfully drafted to avoid political embarrassments, but also because the companies being privatised were in normal trading sectors, non-monopolistic, required no special regulation and did not raise any significant issues for environmentalists, national security, or the protection of the customer.

As a result, the speed of the French programme has been breathtaking. In the first 12 months, nearly 50 per cent of the original five-year privatisation programme was carried out, with total receipts approaching £10 billion. Sales included the glass and industrial products manufacturer, Saint Gobain, Paribas, Crédit Commercial de France, Compagnie Générale d'Électricité, Agence Havas, together with two smaller banks, a telephone manufacturer and a television channel.

Across the Atlantic in the USA, the Reagan administration was keen to follow suit. It had one signal disadvantage in this game: very little to sell. Although the US postal service is nationalised, telecommunications, gas, oil, coal, airlines, the motor industry, the steel industry and shipbuilding were already entirely in the private sector. State governments and local authorities have, of course, provided a large number of services – and the USA has been a leader in contracting these services out to the private sector. But the only major federal government assets in the traditional trading sector were Conrail, Amtrak and the Power Marketing Administration (which is responsible for a relatively small part of US electricity supply). The other potentially saleable assets lay much closer to the heart of government, such as the naval petroleum reserves at Teapot Dome, Wyoming, and Elk Hills, California, and various other pieces of government real estate.

Despite this relative paucity of saleable items, President Reagan decided in 1986 to engage in a privatisation programme which was expanded in the budget speech of 1987 to cover some $20 billion of asset sales, including the naval petroleum reserve, Amtrak and the Power Marketing Administration. The first step was the privatisation of Conrail, which was sold to the public for $1.65 billion in March 1987. In many ways, this was an ideal privatisation candidate: formed in the mid 1970s out of Penn Central and a number of other small railways, it was never profitable until 1981. Fifteen per cent of its shares were already owned by its present and previous employees. Its size, though large by international standards, was small in relation to the total

17

size of the American capital markets. The sale by the federal government of its 85 per cent stake was a great success, with a modest but comforting 12 per cent opening premium going to those who participated in the offer. As well as providing an auspicious start to the Reagan programme, this privatisation has had a marked effect on the reaction of capital markets around the world to freight-rail companies, possibly opening the way to privatisations of similar companies in other countries.

Further north in Canada, another right-of-centre government has also been engaged in an active privatisation programme: Northern Transportation, Canada Development Corporation, Canadian Arsenals, De Havilland Aircraft, CNR Route, Pêcheries Canada, Canadair, Nanisivik Mines, and Teleglobe have all been sold, and the sale of a number of other, much larger Crown corporations is under consideration, including Air Canada and Petro-Canada. If these larger corporations are sold, the federal government's programme will become a major example of privatisation, undoubtedly attracting large numbers of small shareholders and creating very considerable interest across the world. At the time of writing, however, the programme has been relatively low-key, with Teleglobe raising the largest sum, about £200 million, and with the privatisations generally taking the form of sales to existing private sector companies, such as the Montreal-based SNC Group which bought Canadian Arsenals, and Boeing, which bought De Havilland. The scale of the exercise can be measured by the fact that the total proceeds of the federal government's programme up to July 1987 were only about £600 million.

The federal government is not, however, the whole story. Some of the Canadian provinces are also pursuing very considerable privatisation programmes. In Quebec, the government has exhibited considerable interest in contracting-out and other forms of transferring public services to the private sector; in addition, a minister responsible for the privatisation of the province's Crown corporations was appointed, a carefully argued document laying down guidelines was issued in February 1986, and an advisory committee reported in June 1986, recommending that ten industrial Crown corporations should be privatised. In August 1986, the gold and niobium activities of SOQUEM, the province's main mining corporation, were sold by public offer as a self-standing corporation which had been formed out of SOQUEM. The offer brought to light demand of some £200 million for the shares, more or less evenly split between domestic and external markets. In British Columbia, an even more adventurous programme is just beginning, with privatisations planned for large numbers of government services and at least one Crown corporation. An equally exciting programme is developing in Saskatchewan, with a major public sector oil company already floated and a large range of activities under consideration for what the Province's government has christened the 'public participation' drive.

Moving south, the right-wing government in Chile has been conducting a continuous privatisation programme since 1973, using a large variety of methods. Recently, mass privatisations with a distinct element of popular capitalism have entered the picture. The first step was the privatisation of the state pension funds in 1981, which enormously developed local capital markets. Cheap finance for small purchasers has been provided by the government, enabling the sale of the two largest banks to small shareholders, and a large number of companies have been sold in various sectors including telecommunications, steel, fertilisers, explosives and pharmaceuticals. After preliminary sales of assets belonging to ENDESA, the electricity utility, a major public offer of electricity shares has now taken place.

To the east, the government of Mr Özal in Turkey – committed to free enterprise, deregulation and increased competition – has conducted a full-scale study of privatisation, and is now beginning the process in earnest. Under a new law, state-owned enterprises to be sold are transferred to the Public Participation Fund Administration, a small group of dedicated experts who have particular responsibility for privatisation. This group has begun work on the privatisation of companies in the cement industry, telecommunications, tourism and aircraft handling. A long list of further privatisations is expected, and the eventual size of the programme could be very large, since the Turkish economy is dominated by state-owned enterprises.

Pragmatist Governments and Privatisation

The privatisation movement has not, by any means, been restricted to avowedly right-wing governments. In Japan, a government noted for its 'pragmatic' and 'non-ideological' approach has begun what may well prove to be the world's largest privatisation programme. In tune with traditional Japanese methods of conducting business and public policy, this privatisation is being conducted in an extremely methodical fashion. In April 1985, the government produced new legislation for the telecommunications industry, enabling Nippon Telephone & Telegraph (a company whose capitalisation is greater than that of the whole West German equity market) to be established as a self-standing corporation. For almost two years, the government retained 100 per cent of the equity, and the company was not in any real sense privatised, though substantial deregulation allowed private competitors to enter the telecommunications market, offering leased lines. However, in 1986, 12.5 per cent of the government's shareholding was put up for sale. In February 1987 the sale was completed and accompanied by a listing on the Toyko Stock Exchange, with further rounds following. The reason for the relatively small proportion sold is the colossal size of the manoeuvre. The first 12.5 per cent tranche alone raised more than twice the amount paid by British investors for the first half of British Telecom. With sale of shares in Japan Airlines now scheduled, and with divestment of both Japan National Railways and the national tobacco monopoly, JTS, due at some point in the future, it seems possible that Japan's programme, though small relative to the Japanese economy, could eventually come close to matching that of the rest of the world's programme in size.

Another country not noted for the ideological bent of its government, but which has begun a considerable privatisation programme, is Italy. The great state holding company, IRI, has sold shares in airline companies, banking, oil, gas, motor manufacturing and other industries. These privatisations have been undertaken not on the initiative of the state itself, but rather as a result of the commercial management of IRI – a company which has a toe in both private and public sectors. Apart from iron, steel and shipyards (where it dominates the sector), its subsidiaries

20

generally face tough commercial competition from private sector companies and are managed more commercially than state enterprises in many countries. Indeed, IRI's move towards privatisation is really a move back towards its role in the 1930s and 1940s, when it generally took a proportion of the shares in any given concern rather than a 100 per cent stake. With the other state holding companies following IRI's lead, such reversions seem likely to become more widespread in Italy, and, as a result, the balance between public and private sectors will probably have undergone substantial alteration by the end of the decade.

Socialist Governments

Perhaps more surprisingly, privatisation is also spreading to countries with socialist governments. In Spain, for example, sales of government interests in bus manufacturing, sherry, construction, high technology, food manufacturing, banking and other sectors are all under way. Although no mass privatisation involving 'popular capitalism' has taken place, this may well be just round the corner – particularly given the Spanish government's current interest in privatising the major state oil company, INH.

Another socialist government, in New Zealand, has been pursuing an extremely interesting and innovative programme. As in Japan, the government has begun by turning what were previously regarded as mere offshoots of the state into self-standing corporations. This process of corporatisation is in one sense not a privatisation, since the state retains 100 per cent of the voting shares. However, in another sense, it is indeed a form of privatisation, since the debt raised by the new corporations will be from the private sector, and 'equity bonds' (or non-voting shares) are also being sold in the private stock market. The programme is designed to achieve the effects of privatisation without sacrificing the principle of state ownership. Application of the policy has been wide-ranging with 'corporatisations' of telecommunications, forestry, land, coal and other industries, and with the issuing of equity bonds now beginning in the petroleum industry and spreading gradually to the other corporatised assets.

Next door, in Australia, another socialist government has begun a more straightforward privatisation programme. When the Australian Liberal Party announced a privatisation policy in mid-1985, this was met with heavy criticism from senior figures in the socialist government. But, by the end of 1985, there were reports that some members of the Labour Party had admitted to being in favour of limited privatisation. In March 1987, Mr Hawke took the initiative by announcing his intention of selling Australian Airlines as a means of reducing the budget deficit. This was a direct breach of the Australian Labour Party platform and senior figures in the Party took the view that the public sector unions – traditionally loyal Labour supporters – would treat the proposal as a direct attack on their reason for supporting the Party. Eventually the government bowed to pressure, shelving plans for a sale of Australian Airlines. But the issue of privatisation was brought forward at the next Party Conference, and in early 1987, the first project – the sale of Williamstown Dockyard – was announced. Subsequently, there has been a good deal of discussion within the Labour Party, the outcome of which is – at the time of writing – uncertain.

A measure of the extent to which privatisation has broken the bounds of conservatism is its introduction in Mexico, a country which has been dominated since 1929 by the Partido Revolucionario Institucional (PRI). Though traditionally a left-of-centre party, the PRI has taken privatisation to heart. In February 1985, the government announced that it intended to dissolve, liquidate, wind up and transfer a large number of government-owned companies. As a result, some 53 state-owned companies have been liquidated, seven more have been transferred to state governments and major sales to the private sector have taken place, including textile companies, banks (together with subsidiaries and minority investments), mineral companies, tourist operations and motor component factories. Other companies are now following, and the pace of privatisation appears to be increasing. As in Spain, it seems likely that the next step will be a move towards mass privatisation, moving up a gear from the relatively low-key sales which have so far taken place.

The Developing World

The progress of privatisation across the developed world has caught the attention of agencies such as the World Bank, the IFC, the IMF, USAID, the Overseas Development Administration in the UK, the Commonwealth Secretariat, and the United Nations. As less-developed countries' budget deficits and external debt have mounted during the 1970s and early 1980s, these international agencies have been looking above all for means of reducing fiscal demands and increasing the vitality of the private sector. Since 1983, they have become increasingly active in advocating privatisation as a useful tool to achieve such results. Numerous studies have been conducted and others are on the way. Investment banks and other consultants have been paid to assist less-developed countries with their privatisation programmes, and conferences have been held to spread the message.

The current move towards privatisation in the Third World no doubt owes some of its origins to the advocacy by international agencies. In view of the considerable dependence of many less-developed countries on agency funds this is hardly surprising. But international pressure alone is not sufficient to explain the quite remarkable extent of privatisation in the Third World. Since the definition of less-developed countries and the definition of privatisation are matters for judgement rather than science, the number of privatisations completed or under way in these countries is a matter for some debate. However, there have certainly been privatisations of one form or another in Bangladesh, Belize, Bolivia, Cameroon, the Dominican Republic, Honduras, Indonesia, Jamaica, Kenya, Malaysia, Pakistan, Peru, Senegal, Sierra Leone, Sri Lanka, Togo, Tunisia and Zaire. Studies and plans are also under way in Costa Rica, Ecuador, Egypt, Fiji, the Gambia, Grenada, Guatemala, Guyana, Jordan, Kenya, Niger, Nigeria, Panama, Rwanda, Somalia, Swaziland and Zimbabwe. The range of assets being privatised, or under consideration for privatisation, is enormous, including brick and fertiliser plants, rubber plants, sugar mills, bacon-processing plants, textiles, farm implements, petroleum distribution, tuna and tomato canning, water wells, hotels, coal gasification, steel mills, refineries, airlines, engineering, chemicals, communications, toll roads, ports, container operations, edible-oil production, ghee mills, contraceptive sales, rice, fibre and cotton mills, irrigation projects, bus services, newspapers, packaging materials, tobacco enterprises, milk-marketing boards, towel factories, banana fields, electricity utilities, investment banks, saw mills, forestry enterprises, car manufacturing, mining, food processing and fish processing, marble quarrying, gas, bridges, dams, automotive maintenance, grain purchasing, vegetable exports, insurance, seed farms, shipping and shipyards, and sewage. Privatisations in these countries have also taken many different forms. In Cameroon, a rubber plant and sugar mill were put out to management contract. In Sierra Leone, four hotels were leased. Sales of assets to private companies have perhaps been the most usual form, with large numbers undertaken in various countries. And in Jamaica – probably the most adventurous of the less-developed countries to date – two major mass privatisations on the British model (indeed, larger relative to the scale of the market than any undertaken in the developed world) have been carried through.

The World-wide Movement

The specific examples cited here do not by any means constitute a complete list. Interest in privatisation is now virtually a world-wide phenomenon. Privatisations have also occurred or are seriously contemplated in Argentina, Austria, Brazil, Finland, South Korea, the Netherlands, Portugal, Singapore and Sweden. The message has even begun to spread in a modified form to the communist countries: public housing is being sold in Cuba and China; private sector businesses are being encouraged in Hungary; private sector worker co-operatives have taken over radio and TV repair services in the Soviet Union. Whatever one thinks of privatisation, it has arrived on the international scene in no uncertain manner. Almost everywhere, the state, as an owner of industry, is in retreat: the balance which tilted so firmly towards the public sector between the 1940s and 1970s is now tilting equally firmly towards the private sector.

2

WHY PRIVATISE?

Fashion or Policy?

The international trend towards privatisation is much easier to describe than to explain. It cannot be fitted into the traditional picture of policy formation, which begins with agreed objectives and progresses through options to decisions, because in this case there is no single authority with a single set of objectives. Although many different governments are pursuing a similar set of policies, they are doing so for very different reasons.

In the UK, John Moore, the Minister who had special responsibility for privatisation during the mid 1980s, gave one account:

> The Government's privatisation strategy is justified on economic and business criteria as well as making sense in political terms. If the present momentum is maintained, it will help provide a remedy for some of the ills that have beset UK industrial performance in recent years... Managers are set free to manage and new opportunities are opened up ... pay bargaining can be carried out much more responsibly and easily... It also enables pride in work and job satisfaction to be increased ... it forces into sharp relief a distinction between activities which are commercial and activities which are not (*Why Privatise?*, Conservative Political Centre, London, 1983).

The explanation given by a French commentator, Jean Loyrette ('Remarques sur le problème des dénationalisations', quoting from paper presented to UNIR conference, May 1985) –

25

drawn from the various statements of the leaders of the right in France before the Chirac government came to power – was somewhat different:

> First objective: reduce the burdens of the Exchequer and reduce the state's budget deficit. Second objective: consolidate the social and political grip of capitalism by building up popular capitalism. Third objective: make the economy more competitive. Fourth objective: reduce the interference of politics in the workings of commerce. Fifth objective: bring workers into share ownership.

The top five priorities listed in order by a survey carried out among senior figures in the Turkish government hint at yet another, overlapping but different, understanding of the reasons for privatisation: to allow market forces to stimulate the economy; to increase productivity and efficiency; to increase quality, quantity, and diversity of the goods and services; to promote widespread share ownership and to speed up the development of the capital markets.

These differences between one country and another are not surprising. Only the most dogmatic political theorists would assume that different governments, with their different circumstances and traditions, would all be pursuing the policy for the same reason. Just as countries join the European Community or run up fiscal deficits for different reasons, so they have a multitude of different reasons for privatising.

The interesting point – and one which is rather more surprising – is the near impossibility of attributing a clear or definite aim to any one of the governments that have been involved in privatisation. At the beginning of a privatisation programme, most governments have a welter of different aims, not least because the various departments have quite different concerns. In theory, the aims of each department should be fairly predictable: a treasury or finance ministry should be wanting to reduce fiscal deficits and decrease the national debt; the department of industry should be wanting to increase the operational efficiency of the businesses; the department of trade should be wanting to increase competition and reduce economic distortions; the department of employment should be wanting to spread employee involvement. But in practice, the patterns are rarely if ever, so simple. Departments have their own battles to fight and frequently have long-term programmes into which privatisation fits as a mere piece in a jigsaw. Moreover, particular politicians, each with their own beliefs and ambitions, have aims for themselves and for the country at large which transcend the particular post that they happen to be occupying at any given moment. Searching in all these cross-currents for a single stream of thought is dangerously naive and unproductive. Far better to admit that within any government the reasons for privatising – like the reasons against privatising – will be many and various at any given time. And they will vary not only in relation to the differing aims of differing actors but also in relation to different forms of privatisation. The contracting-out of a local service and the sale of a major public utility are both labelled 'privatisation', and rightly; but it would be close to irrational for anyone to assume that these two very different moves could achieve the same aims or be done for the same purpose.

The aims of privatisation also change as programmes proceed. The British government's emphasis on the benefits for business efficiency, manifest in John Moore's 1983 speech quoted above, had shifted two years later. Speaking in 1985, John Moore said that privatisation policies had 'been specifically designed to further a number of objectives'. Of these, 'greater efficiency' was only one. In addition, he argued that the policies aimed to 'reduce the role of the public sector and provide substantial sale receipts. They allow employees to take a direct stake in the companies in which they work . . . And, importantly, they provide a major stimulus to wider share ownership' ('The Success of Privatisation', speech, 17 July 1985). By 1986, the emphasis in the UK was being firmly placed on the last of these aims – popular capitalism and the ownership of shares by the ordinary man – as a further speech by John Moore faithfully reflects:

Our programme, which is already succeeding even beyond the dreams of the optimists, is directed towards the three key areas of life: homes, work-places, and the wider community. We are extending home ownership, increasing employee participation

27

in the ownership of their companies and spreading the ownership of public companies to millions of ordinary people (*The Value of Ownership*, Conservative Political Centre, London, 1986).

The conclusion must be that there is no single or simple answer to the question 'Why do governments privatise?' There are, however, some central reasons, most of which have been given as explanations by proponents of privatisation in most of the countries involved – though with different emphases and at different stages of their privatisation programmes:

1. The effect on the nature of government.
2. The effect on operational efficiency.
3. The effect on fiscal deficits and national debt.
4. The effect on subsidies and distortions.
5. The effect on regulation and deregulation.
6. The attraction of overseas capital.
7. The effect on the domestic capital market.
8. The effect on employee involvement.
9. The effect on the social and political landscapes.

At first sight, these reasons for privatisation appear to have little or no connection with one another. This impression is in one sense correct: there are, for example, great differences in practice between a privatisation which is undertaken primarily to reduce the fiscal deficit and one which is undertaken primarily to eliminate subsidies. In the first case, the government will seek to maximise current receipts by leaving intact long-term benefits which the company being privatised had been receiving from the state; whereas, in the second case, the government will reduce its immediate receipts by depriving the company of subsidies and other benefits in advance of privatisation. Such conflicts of interest can, however, easily be overplayed. There is, underlying the reasons commonly given for privatisation, if not a general theory at least a general theme – namely, distrust of the state as a manager of commercial enterprise. The proponent of privatisation begins with the supposition that, all other things being equal, it is likely that the state will not be a good manager of any given commercial entity; in each particular case, he looks for the specific advantages which a specific privatisation could bring, and these become his reasons for that particular privatisation – in one instance, the reduction of subsidy and distortion; in another, an immediate financial advantage for the exchequer; and so on.

Effect on the Nature of Government

Probably the most important but least understood reason given for engaging in privatisation is the effect that a transfer of ownership from the state to the private sector can have upon the nature of government. This aspect of privatisation is frequently ignored by the commentators, who concentrate almost exclusively on financial and economic effects and thereby ignore the fact that privatisation is in origin a political rather than an economic or financial act. The decision to privatise is made by politicians and administrators, not by businessmen or financiers – it is, in other words, made by people whose primary concern is with the role of government and the formation of public policy. One should not, therefore, be surprised that the wish to change the operation of government is frequently one of the main motives of a privatiser.

When an industry is owned by the state, politicians and administrators become indirectly responsible for its performance. They have to appoint its board, they have to answer for it in the legislature, and – most important – they have to stand behind it, guaranteeing any losses and providing any funding. As a result, ministers cannot be indifferent to the fate of a nationalised industry. They are bound to concern themselves with its operations, its investment decisions, its balance sheet and its returns. Almost inevitably, the department or departments which are responsible for the industry begin to identify with its interests and ministers and officials begin to feel personally responsible for its performance. As the years go by, the number of past decisions for which ministers and officials are genuinely responsible grows, and the feeling of personal responsibility increases. With this increasingly strong responsibility comes an increasing concern to ensure that the industry performs well – and hence an increasing identification with the interests of the industry.

This process can have significant effects on the way in which public policy is discussed within departments and on the outcome of those discussions. During the 1960s and 1970s in Britain, the extent to which departments of state came to think of themselves as the guardian of 'their' nationalised industries was truly remarkable. The 'sponsoring' department for a particular industry frequently fought long and hard battles to ensure that 'their' industries received adequate funding from the Exchequer and frequently acted in concert with senior management to promote policies favourable to the industry. And this is not merely a British phenomenon. Any connoisseur of the world's bureaucracies will testify to the presence of similar patterns in country after country.

The most striking example of this tendency is to be found in the airline industry. The national airline is perhaps the most common of all forms of nationalised industry. In 1984, non-communist Europe alone contained a large number of airlines which were more than 50 per cent government-owned, including British Airways, Air France, Lufthansa (West Germany), Alitalia (Italy), TAP (Portugal), Sabena (Belgium), Iberia (Spain), THY (Turkey), and SAS (Denmark, Norway and Sweden). In the USA, by contrast, there were no nationalised airlines whatsoever. As a result, the attitudes of governments in the USA and Europe have been absolutely what one would have expected. In the USA, air fares have been low and massive deregulation has lowered them further. In Europe, where each ministry of transport has been defending the interests of its own airline, deregulation has proved almost impossible to achieve and air fares remain high. One could hardly have a clearer example of the way in which the relationship between nationalised industries and their sponsoring ministries can tilt the attention of ministers and officials away from the interests of the consumer and towards consulting the interests of the industries themselves.

This feature of nationalised industries does not hit the headlines, partly because it does not generate much newsworthy dispute. Officials and management typically come closer together as time progresses and there appears to be a harmony of policy which attracts little or no public attention. The pattern does, however, frequently attract the attention of those politicians who are in any case inclined to be distrustful of the state's ability to run industry. Indeed, it usually comes very forcefully to their attention because it proves one of the major obstacles to achieving other goals which such ministers usually have. When any government favours deregulation, wishes to promote the interests of consumers and wants to cut public spending, it frequently comes face to face with an officialdom intent on the very reverse because of the sponsoring role taken up *vis-à-vis* the nationalised industries.

Part of the point of privatisation for such governments is to alter this position – to remove close links and the identification of interest between departments and particular industries. The extent to which this will actually work in practice still remains to be seen. Certainly, one cannot expect a complete transformation: agriculture ministries around the world have been protecting and subsidising the interests of farmers for years without any significant nationalisation, and there are plenty of effective private sector lobbyists who persuade government departments to identify the interests of the state with those of a particular industry. However, privatisation does remove three great causes of the problem: it ends the responsibility of the minister and officials for the performance of the industry in the eyes of the legislature, or at any rate dramatically lessens this sense of responsibility; it ends the role of the state as financier for the industry, and hence leaves investment decisions to the company itself and to the financial marketplace rather than to officials; and it distances the state from decisions about appointment of the board. This makes it reasonable for the proponents of privatisation to guess – even if they cannot in every case be sure – that public policy will be discussed in a different and rather more congenial way by ministers and officials in departments which have lost 'their' nationalised industries to the private sector. It is difficult to find documented public statements of this attitude, but it is something frequently, if privately, expressed in the corridors of power by many of those who are responsible for privatisation in the UK and elsewhere. It also forms one of the standard arguments put forward by academics and ginger groups when proposing privatisation. Sir Alfred Sherman, formerly head of the British Centre for Policy Studies, gives a vivid description of what such proponents see as the problem:

On entering office, the Minister is bound to be faced by a crisis in all 'his' industrial undertakings, since they are by their nature in permanent crisis. He will be urged by his advisers to give more money to keep them going, 'while things can be sorted out'. It then transpires that losses are higher than envisaged – they always are. A new chairman is sought, who must be given a chance. His terms of reference are in essence: 'Go on running it while we work out what to do, but try to do so more efficiently', whatever that may mean. But, of course, it will not be managed more efficiently, for all the reasons underlying its establishment in the first place. The choice is between hiving off and closing down, on the one hand, or facing losses which increase by their own momentum, on the other. More money is requested. Union promises are made, *in extremis*, and broken as soon as the next tranche is forthcoming. . . It is like a bad film re-made time and time again with different actors. And to these momentous decisions, where mistakes can intensify Britain's vicious circle of decline and confrontation, are devoted only a corner of a Minister's time and mind, serviced by officials who are partisan. Nationalisation is an extension of politics by other means. . . It follows that, insofar as it is possible to break up nationalised companies into independent units, and sell off any that can find customers, both expedients decrease the political strength of what remains, thereby decreasing its ability to exact tribute (*The Crisis Calls for a Minister of Denationalisation*, AIMS, London, undated).

Effect on Operational Efficiency

If the effect of privatisation on the nature of government is important to the politicians and the political theorists, it is the other side of the coin – the effect on the company itself – that mainly occupies the attention of the financial community. Indeed, for many commentators – albeit not for the most sophisticated – this constitutes the only real test of the success or failure of privatisation. 'The question' is often taken to be whether a company will perform more or less efficiently when moved from state ownership into the private sector.

The advocates of privatisation have strong, though by no means overwhelming, grounds for believing that, all else being equal, a move to the private sector will tend to increase efficiency. They argue that the disciplines of the financial marketplace, the need to provide returns on capital that will satisfy investors, are a far stronger, more continuous and more economically rational check on a company's performance than the often inconsistent investment and lending policy of the government which may well be dictated more by short-term political necessity than by long-term economic rationality. They add that, from the point of view of the company itself, the combination of access to private sector funding and the need to achieve adequate returns is likely to make managers focus on cost control, responsibility to the customer, commercial advantage and the economic case for any specific investment. Finally, they argue that a company in the private sector is more likely to have a sensible and efficient personnel policy, with senior managers paid whatever is necessary to achieve the best results, unencumbered by inappropriate comparisons against civil service salaries, and with no mother state to take care of the consequences of restrictive union practices and unsustainably high unit costs.

There is no doubt that these arguments and others like them have played an important part in bringing about privatisation. The idea that nationalised industries will prosper and become more efficient runs through many of the statements made by politicians about the reasons for the policy. Indeed it was present from the start, in the first liberal economic proposals for privatisation put forward in the UK during the 1970s. Dr Rhodes Boyson, for example, wrote in 1971 that:

The economic record of the nationalised industries judged by the return on capital invested is about one-third of that of private industry, despite the periodic and massive writing-down of capital in the nationalised concerns. Between 1959 and 1964, the return on capital of the nationalised Richard Thomas and Baldwin firms in the steel industry was well below that of the denationalised steel firms. Between 1951 and 1964 the average price rise of the products of the nationalised indus-ries was 95 per cent yet in private manufacturing industries

33

the increase averaged only 18 per cent over the same period ('The Rise and Fall of a Myth' in R. Boyson, ed., *Goodbye to Nationalisation*, Churchill Press, London, 1971).

The implication is clear: privatise, and efficiency will almost automatically increase. But is this right? Is it true that nationalised industries perform better when moved to the private sector?

There is evidence to support the thesis. Some of it is anecdotal. One of the senior administrators of British Telecom, for example, has described the radical shift since privatisation in the way British Telecom goes about making capital investment decisions: according to his account, the company before privatisation asked itself how much money it would be allowed to raise in a given year, and spent it on the various projects favoured by its engineers; after privatisation, by contrast, he reports that alternative investment strategies are examined to determine which will have the best effect on the net present value of the corporation. In a similar vein, there has been an academic investigation into the efficiency of private industries compared with those in the public sector, contained in reports written by David G. Davies and published in the *Journal of Law and Economics*: 'The Efficiency of Public versus Private Firms: The Case of Australia's Two Airlines' (vol. 14, April 1971) and 'Property Rights and Economic Efficiency: The Australian Airlines Revisited' (vol. 20, April 1977). In these reports Davies compared the performance of the government-owned Trans Australian Airlines (TAA) and the privately owned Australian National Airway (Ansett). The two airlines had very similar operations. Their passenger and freight rates were identical; routes, specific ports of call and frequency of flights were similar; indeed, both airlines typically had identical departure times over the same routes. Government employees divided their flights equally between the two airlines and the freight services were allocated equally to each airline. Both airlines provided the same capacity and the same number of aircraft over the routes. Davies tested three measures of productivity: freight and mail tonnage carried per employee, passengers carried per employee, and revenue earned per employee. These variables were observed annually over a ten-year period from 1958–9 to 1968–9 and the results were updated through to 1973–4. Throughout the

34

investigation Ansett (the private airline) showed significantly higher productivity than TAA in every one of the three measures tested.

Other evidence comes from the contrasting record of public and private municipal services. Notable examples of savings in the UK are given in Table 1. The British Audit Commission, which monitors efficiency in local government, has studied comparative efficiency in privatised and non-privatised refuse collection. The Commission concludes that even the worst performances achieved by privatised refuse collection systems are substantially better than those typically achieved in local authorities where privatisation has not occurred. This view is beginning to be accepted by a large range of British local government officials and is held even by some elected members whose political position does not dispose them favourably towards privatisation.

A prominent transport consultant in the USA estimates that cost savings in the privatised US bus services have ranged from 10 to 60 per cent, and quotes the following examples:

- In Los Angeles, three large contracts have recently been awarded, with savings of from 37 to 50 per cent.
- In Houston, the private park and ride service is operated for 33 per cent less than public costs.
- In Seattle, a private express service is operated for 37 per cent less than the previous public costs.
- In Chicago, privately provided service for the disabled is operated at cost savings of more than 50 per cent (Wendell Cox, 'Privatisation in the Public Services', paper presented at the Fraser Institute Conference on Privatisation, Vancouver, 24 July 1987).

A Canadian expert reveals that a similar pattern was observable when refuse collection was privatised in a Canadian locality (Table 2). The experience in Japanese cities appears to be the same (Table 3).

This evidence is, however, by no means conclusive. There is no absolute scientific control, since the same industry or service is by necessity not at the same moment under private and public ownership and any differences can therefore always be attributed

35

TABLE 1   SAVINGS FROM PRIVATISATION OF MUNICIPAL
SERVICES

Local authority	Operation	Annual saving £
Bath City	Public lavatory, street cleaning and refuse collection	300,000
Bromley Borough Council	Street cleaning	200,000
Chiltern District Council	Refuse collection	160,000
Ealing Borough Council	Street cleaning	600,000
Eastbourne Borough Council	Street cleaning and refuse collection	500,000
Kensington and Chelsea Council	Refuse collection	100,000
Mendip Borough Council	Refuse collection	126,000
Milton Keynes Borough Council	Refuse collection	488,000
North Norfolk District Council	Refuse collection	175,000
Southend-on-Sea Borough Council	Street cleaning and refuse collection	600,000
Tamworth District Council	Refuse collection	200,000
Vale of White Horse District Council	Street cleaning and refuse collection	290,000
Wirral Borough Council	Street cleaning and refuse collection	1,400,000

Source: M. Pirie, *Privatisation in Theory and Practice*, Adam Smith Institute.

TABLE 2   COST OF AND PRODUCTIVITY LEVELS IN REFUSE
COLLECTION IN RICHMOND, CANADA, BEFORE PRIVATISATION
(1980–2) AND AFTER (1983)

	Cost per household (C$)	Total households served	Total collected (tonnes)	Tonnes per crew member per day
1980	42.71	25,007	24,772	5.29
1981	52.27	25,456	19,438	5.79
1982	52.71	25,731	24,985	6.20
1983	31.72	26,141	26,232	10.25

Source: James McDavid, 'Privatisation in Local Governments in Canada', paper delivered to the Fraser Institute Conference on Privatisation, Vancouver, 24 July 1987.

to third-party causes. There are, in addition, a number of apparent counter-examples – including a number of management buyouts in the UK, such as Brooke Marine, Swan Hunter and Vospers, and also BCRIC in British Columbia. These are companies which have gone bankrupt or performed badly once in the private sector. Moreover, the differences between private and public sector municipal services may well be due to the introduction of competition rather than to privatisation. And there has already been considerable criticism of the levels of service provided by some privatised monopolies, such as British Telecom in the UK.

The advocates of privatisation are not, therefore, in a position to claim (and have not generally claimed) that the mere act of privatisation will guarantee increased operational efficiency. Instead, they have to rely on a collection of necessarily inconclusive arguments and evidence to back their fundamental feeling that bureaucrats are in the long run likely to manage enterprises less well than the private sector. As with most really big questions of policy, this is ultimately a matter of judgement rather than a matter of science.

37

TABLE 3   PERFORMANCE RESULTS OF CONTRACTING-OUT IN
JAPANESE CITIES

	Effect of contracting out (% of response)				
	Efficiency up	Cost down	Staff down	Staff up	Service up
Governmental office services					
Cleaning	78.3	57.4	67.1	11.9	59.0
Security	65.7	47.0	62.9	14.5	37.0
Elevator maintenance	71.7	43.0	53.8	12.5	68.4
Heating and cooling	67.4	47.7	65.8	8.8	44.3
Telephone switchboard operations	64.7	82.9	86.5	6.5	54.7
Information service	70.7	59.0	74.2	9.7	74.2
Shorthand (steno)	89.1	45.1	64.7	9.1	46.8
Resident registration records	84.4	68.2	68.2	4.5	65.9
Typing	82.2	78.4	84.3	3.1	46.5
Printing	80.6	40.7	58.1	9.1	64.1
Computing services					
Tax assessment	97.6	58.4	70.1	11.6	76.4
Tax collection	96.7	58.3	71.1	7.4	73.4
Payroll processing	98.1	51.6	71.3	9.3	35.7
Various statistical tasks	99.1	25.8	57.0	15.1	54.5
Other services					
Human waste	85.6	58.3	70.5	6.7	68.6
Sewage charges	83.1	68.1	86.1	1.4	60.6

TABLE 3   PERFORMANCE RESULTS OF CONTRACTING-OUT IN
JAPANESE CITIES—CONTD.

	Effect of contracting out (% of response)				
	Efficiency up	Cost down	Staff down	Staff up	Service up
Water charges	82.8	65.3	86.4	2.4	55.4
Citizen awareness surveys	65.9	10.8	37.3	9.6	53.7
Water meter reading	74.2	72.6	87.3	1.8	35.6
Design of public facilities	84.1	33.6	42.9	17.4	39.3
Surveying and mapping of roads	85.8	25.5	43.0	16.2	54.3
Publications distribution	80.4	35.6	60.8	13.6	68.4
Home services for disabled	60.0	31.1	50.4	6.4	82.2
Overall average	80.3	50.6	66.1	9.1	57.3

Source: J.T. Marlin, Editor in chief, *Privatisation of Local Government Activities, Lessons from Japan,* The National Civics League, New York, 1982.

Effect on Fiscal Deficits and National Debt

Privatisation is of course, not merely a political and economic policy. It is also a financial transaction. In many privatisations, the amount of money changing hands is small and the financial benefits for government are intangible and long delayed. The British government's gift of Hoverspeed to its employees for £1 is a case in point: the immediate receipts were effectively nil and the long-term financial benefits for the government (possibly avoiding subsidies which would otherwise have to be paid) are difficult to assess. In contracting out of services – possibly the single most common form of privatisation around the world – the government

39

(whether central, provincial or local) typically receives no immediate cash payment whatsoever. On the contrary, the government makes a payment to the new private contractor for the provision of services which otherwise have been comfortably disguised as part of a departmental budget. Any savings which accrue – however considerable in the long term – are visible only when a comparison is made between the cost that would have been incurred if the service had been provided by public employees and its costs under the new private sector managers. These forms of privatisation are, in effect, for the current account: they gradually decrease running costs and thereby almost invisibly reduce pressure on fiscal deficits. Like any government exercise in cutting recurrent costs, their effects on budgets are slow and steady.

Major sales of state assets, on the other hand, have a direct, immediate and easily ascertainable effect on fiscal balances and the national debt. Each such sale is, in practice, a method of capitalising a future stream of revenues which would otherwise have accrued gradually. In the case of the largest sales such as the French government's disposal of Paribas ($4 billion), the British government's disposal of British Gas (total receipts $12 billion) and the Japanese government's sale of NTT shares (approximately $15 billion) the immediate budgetary impact can be enormous. The total government receipts for the British Gas sale, for example, were equivalent to approximately 4 per cent of public expenditure for the 1986–7 financial year. It seems likely that, as the scale of the privatisation programme in several countries increases, several governments around the world will receive bonuses of this kind – a capitalisation of latent wealth which closely resembles the effects of selling licences to exploit oil, gas or some other natural resource.

Before the British government embarked on its now massive programme, the scale of these effects was not anticipated. Exponents of asset sales may well have thought that they would be able to garner some useful small sums and to reduce the call of the nationalised industries on the public purse – though evidence even of these aims is scarce. The scale of the disposal – which was at the time regarded as unthinkable by many commentators – changed perceptions of what was possible by showing that in developed capital markets sums could be raised that were large even by comparison with fiscal arithmetic. Since this discovery, the news of which spread rapidly throughout the world due to the high profile achieved by the British government in the sale of British Telecom, there is no doubt that reducing deficits has become an important motive for governments to engage in privatisation. This is particularly true in less-developed countries where deficits and consequent overseas debts are a matter of urgent concern. For a government with a low credit rating and rapidly escalating debts, large-scale privatisation can appeal like a pool of water far off in the Sahara – possibly a mirage and requiring a journey fraught with danger, but irresistibly attractive.

The reduction of the deficit has certainly been one of the major reasons for Jamaica's privatisation programme, with aggregate receipts equalling roughly 5 per cent of annual public expenditure or 15 per cent of the current deficit. Further up the scale of economic development, the governments of British Columbia and of Israel, which are both struggling to reduce deficits, have seen this as a powerful reason for constructing a far-reaching privatisation programme, and are setting about the task with vigour. Where this motive is present, it can have startling effects on the speed and scale of privatisation. As the British example shows, the Treasury's desire to raise a large amount of cash quickly can keep up pressure to privatise even those industries whose strategic and monopolistic position makes sales intrinsically complicated to achieve. Once the anticipated proceeds are written into the budget, failure to realise them becomes a cause of serious financial embarrassment for the government. This keeps up the impetus at times when the will might otherwise flag in the face of difficulties and complications.

Effect on Subsidies and Distortions

Privatisation can also be a tool for bringing into the open previously hidden financial relationships between the government and a nationalised industry. All over the world, the performance of nationalised industry is economically distorted by some form of hidden subsidy or hidden penalty. There are several common forms of such subsidies and penalties. The first is hidden controls

41

on output pricing. Frequently, a nationalised industry provides goods or services which are politically sensitive. Under such circumstances, the government has an interest in ensuring that the price of the goods or services does not rise too fast, and – as the shareholder of the industry – the government is in a position to ensure that this political demand is met virtually regardless of the effect on the industry's profitability. If the government owns 100 per cent of the equity and chooses either to accept reduced returns or to find some other means of artificially increasing the returns, no individual has a direct cause for complaint. There is consequently endless room for manoeuvre, and governments across the world have made good use of this. Typically, fares on nationalised rail, bus and ferry services have been kept artificially low; that is, below the levels at which the industries are capable of achieving returns on capital equivalent to those that would be demanded in the private sector. The same is often true of nationalised utilities, especially where these are used as an invisible subsidy for another industry whose economic health is fragile. Hydro-electric utilities in Canada, for example, have been used to provide power at well below market rates, giving other Canadian industries – such as the pulp and paper sector – an edge over the international competition.

A second form of subsidy or penalty is artificial supply pricing. Governments often artificially adjust the prices paid by national- ised industries for raw materials in order to administer a hidden subsidy for the provider of that material. The 'joint understand- ing' between the Central Electricity Generating Board and Brit- ish Coal in the UK is a case in point: the agreement forces the CEGB to buy British coal, even though this is produced at prices well above world levels, in order to keep open a large number of deep coal mines which would otherwise have to be either subsi- dised directly or closed.

The third form of subsidy or penalty is hidden transfers within an industry. Sometimes, the items which the government would wish to see produced at an artificially low price constitute part rather than the whole of the produce of a given nationalised industry. In such cases (which frequently occur, for example, in relation to rural transport and energy provision) intrinsically profitable business units within the industry can be used to cross-subsidise those items which are subject to artificial pricing. In some cases, the extent of cross-subsidisation, involving transfer payments, intra-company liabilities, artificial supply and off-take contracts between business units, and so on, can be very great. In some nationalised industries, intra-company dealings are positively labyrinthine, making the accounting systems of the parent companies almost impossible to follow.

Privatisation is frequently seen by its exponents within government as a means of exposing, clarifying and if possible eliminating these hidden subsidies and distortions. When a nationalised industry, or part of a nationalised industry, moves into the private sector new commercial rules apply. Private investors cannot be expected to accept unpredictable and artifically low output pricing. Nor will the company, once in the private sector, be willing to purchase goods or services from other nationalised industries at artificial rates. And where a component of a nationalised industry is being privatised, investors in that component will not accept its being used as a supply ship or subsidy machine for the remainder of the industry. The government is, therefore, forced to examine the various transfer payments and subsidies, and to construct explicit contracts or agreements with which the private investor will feel comfortable. When the Caribbean Cement Company was privatised in Jamaica, for example, a new long-term supply contract had to be drawn up between the company and Jamaica Gypsum and Quarries Ltd, the principal supplier of gypsum, to formalise arrangements which had previously been made *ad hoc*. And when the Royal Ordnance Factories were privatised in the UK, investors and analysts placed great weight on the amendments of the Explosives and Propellants Agreement which governed supply from the company to the Ministry of Defence.

Effect on Regulation

The most striking example of the way in which privatisation can make explicit what was previously submerged is the regulation of utilities. Where a nationalised utility, such as an electricity or gas provider, a water company, a telephone company or even an airport, is privatised, the government cannot allow the prices charged to the customer to be governed by pure commercial logic, since such a utility – even if it faces elements of competition – will almost always be sufficiently dominant to exert a monopoly rent if it is not explicitly controlled. So long as the utility is nationalised, the government is able to respond to this problem through *ad hoc* pricing decisions; but once the utility is privatised, some clear, statutory form of regulation is required so that both customers and investors are protected.

Utility privatisation outside the UK has only just begun. The privatisation of Nippon Telephone and Telegraph in Japan and of the Carribean Cement Company in Jamaica are the only large-scale examples completed to date. However, several governments are currently engaged in serious programmes to privatise their utilities, including those of Singapore, Chile, Malaysia, and British Columbia. In all these places, regulation is high on the agenda and it is likely that new explicit regulatory systems will be devised to achieve a proper balance between the interests of the customer and the interests of the investor.

In this field, as in many other aspects of privatisation, the UK has led the way. With massive telephone and gas utilities already privatised, and with water and electricity well on the way, a great deal of sophisticated attention has been given to regulation, and the government has certainly regarded the creation of suitable, explicit regulatory systems as one of its principal aims. As is by now well known, the UK has avoided the unpredictable and opaque form of regulation applied to utilities such as the telephone companies in the USA, and has instead established formulae which link the average price charged by a utility to the general index of retail prices, with allowances for increases in the cost of inputs and with a special drive for efficiency which is achieved by allowing the utility to raise its prices by less than the average for retail prices each year.

The details of these formulae are extremely complicated, but the general principles are absolutely clear, can be explained to the public at large, and control directly the prices charged – which are the items of most immediate interest to the consumer. There have, of course, been some complaints from various parties about the specific operation of the formulae, but the general reception has been good and their operation has eliminated the long-running complaints generated by *ad hoc* ministerial decisions on pricing when the industries were still nationalised.

Effect on Competition

Many of the governments which favour privatisation are also strong proponents of increasing competition. This is no accident: competition is after all, far more frequently found in the private than in the public sector. Indeed, every private sector company, whatever its underlying commercial position, is bound to compete in at least one respect, since it must attract private equity and private debt in competition with other potential investments and borrowers. This form of competition is at least as important as commercial competition, since it provides a natural method of rationing capital and hence of directing national resources to those areas where returns are highest. It is, in fact, the counterpart of the point about operational efficiency: privatised companies are pushed towards efficiency because of the disciplines by competition imposed in the financial marketplace.

Some proponents of privatisation also used to argue that true competition is nearly impossible in any sector where a nationalised industry has a major stake, since the nationalised company can appeal to the state's bottomless purse to fund any losses that may occur – with the result that predatory pricing is always an option. However, the history of bus deregulation in the UK and of the contracting-out of services in the USA has shown that if sufficient attention is paid to constructing appropriate contractual and tendering arrangements, private sector commercial competition can be brought to bear on nationalised services even where those nationalised services are in receipt of subsidy. More recently, experience in Northern Ireland, involving the construction of a private sector alternative to nationalised power stations, has shown that the same principles can probably apply even in an industry where capital expenditure is high and the nationalised sector has large sunk costs. The argument has, therefore, moved on, with the exponents of privatisation maintaining that the private sector can be used as a stimulus for competition even where a nationalised industry remains *in situ*.

Interestingly, in the UK there are increasing anxieties about service levels in those privatisations which have left commercial monopolies intact, even where tough price regulation has been installed. Powerful feelings of this sort have been expressed by free-traders who might have otherwise been expected to favour privatisation. In a recent article in the *Daily Telegraph* (31 July 1987), Ferdinand Mount, the former head of the British Prime Minister's Policy Unit, put the case strongly: 'All in all, it has been a rotten month for the reputation of the privatised monopoly. It is becoming increasingly clear that the regulators have no teeth and the operators no conscience'. In an introduction to a major work on privatisation, three major academic commentators, John Kay, Colin Mayor and David Thompson, put the same point equally strongly:

Privatisation policy in the UK has increasingly come to empha-sise the virtues of denationalisation . . . denationalisation now appears to take precedence over, or even to be carried out at the expense of, the promotion of competition. The conflict between privatisation and liberalisation is no longer a conflict but a rout. We do not believe that the change of policy direction is supported by the empirical evidence on the relative perform-ance of public and private enterprise. This stresses the role of competition and supports scepticism about the value of de-nationalisation outside a competitive environment (*Privatisa-tion and Regulation*, Oxford University Press, Oxford, 1986).

There is evidence that, in the UK at least, these arguments are now being taken seriously by the government, whilst privatisation has come to be seen increasingly as an opportunity for creating a degree of competition which would not otherwise have occurred. In particular, ministers have made it clear that they intend to introduce strong elements of competition into the electricity industry when it is privatised, and this may well become a precedent for future utility privatisation in other countries.

Effect on Employee Involvement

One of the most surprising, and at the same time one of the most important, aspects of privatisation has been its use as a vehicle for bringing employees into ownership of the companies for which they work. The spread of employee ownership under privatisation has been truly remarkable in the UK. In most of the biggest privatisations, over 90 per cent of the workforce have taken shares, often owning as much as 10 per cent of the company after privatisation; there have been special incentives for employees in all the public offers; and there have, in addition, been almost 30 management or employee buyouts.

The case of British Telecom is just one illustration of the lengths to which the British government has gone to encourage employee share participation. The government offered 54 ordinary shares (worth £70.20 at the offer for sale price) to each employee, *free of charge*; a *matching offer* of two ordinary shares given without charge to an employee, in respect of each share purchased by that employee up to a maximum of 77 shares; and a *priority offer* of shares for employees and British Telecom Superannuation Scheme pensioners, under which each eligible person could apply for shares on a special priority form and was entitled to a discount of 10 per cent on the offer for sale price if shares were held continuously until the date when the final instalment was payable. In addition, the company set up at the time of privatisation an employee share save scheme under which an employee making monthly contributions out of his wage packet is entitled to share options; and a share option scheme under which directors and other senior employees are given options to purchase shares in the normal way. The effect of these various measures was impressive. Some 222,000 employees (about 96 per cent of the workforce) took free shares. Of these, 182,000 also bought matching shares. And the signs are that a very large number of these shares will continue to be held: of the 62,000 employees who also bought shares under the priority offer, and who were free to sell immediately, 59,000 (95 per cent) still retained their shares in June 1986. In addition, over 80,000 employees took up options under the employee share save scheme in 1985.

In Jamaica, at the opposite end of the spectrum in terms of size, similar results have been achieved. A complex scheme of incentives and protections was devised and roughly 13 per cent of the shares offered in the National Commercial Bank were reserved for its employees, almost all of whom participated in the offer. Similar effects have also been noticed in other countries, including Turkey, where the involvement of employees is officially classed as one of the prime aims of privatisation. To fulfil this aim, the Turkish government has undertaken a special study of employee ownership, and it seems likely that privatisations in Turkey will include a large element of employee participation. Meanwhile, in France, the trend is already well established, with employees taking major stakes in all of the privatisations so far conducted.

What makes this feature of privatisation particularly interesting is that it constitutes a stealing of the clothes of the left by the right. It appeals to precisely the same sentiments as those which generated the co-operative movement – the desire to give workers a piece of the companies for which they work. But it achieves this by capitalist rather than socialist methods. The result is that, instead of a company moving out of the capital markets and into a permanent co-operative with no access to external investment, the privatised companies, which have either been bought out by management and employees or in which employees hold a significant stake, remain able to attract funds from the normal financial marketplace. Politicians of the right have not been slow to see the long-term advantages of such a transformation. They now see employee participation as one of the most attractive features of privatisation – an element to be emphasised as much as possible. It should not, however, be assumed that this was the intention from the start. It arose more as a discovery than as an invention: in the early British privatisations, the employees were seen merely as a useful source of capital; the political importance of employee involvement only became apparent once the level of employee enthusiasm became evident and the potential for stealing the clothes of the opposition was realised. Once the way had been shown in the UK, other governments saw the point and followed the lead. An interesting example of international follow-my-leader.

Effect on the Capital Market

Another unexpected development has been the extraordinary broadening of the capital markets under the influence of privatisation. In the UK, there were 2 million shareholders in 1979, before privatisation started. There are now estimated to be nearly 9 million, almost as many as there are trade unionists. Like the spread of employee involvement, this 'popular capitalism' has had dramatic political effects, turning private industry and the stock market into something of interest and immediate concern to a large section of the population which previously regarded investment as an arcane matter suitable only for financiers and the rich. Once again, similar effects have occurred in other countries, with the number of investors in France increasing from 1.5 million to 5.5 million, and share ownership more than tripling in Jamaica. Privatisation has, in other words, become a vehicle for transforming the breadth of stock markets across the world. And not only the breadth. The depth of the markets is also being vastly enhanced with a dramatic increase in the equity portfolios of financial institutions and the total capitalisation of markets. Between the beginning of 1980 and early August 1987, the total capitalisation of the London Stock Exchange rose by some 700 per cent; over the same period, the total capitalisation of the New York Stock Exchange rose by only 230 per cent. A large part of this difference is, of course, due to the different performance of stock prices in the two markets and the liberalisation of financial services in the UK; but it seems reasonable to suppose that the release of over £15 billion of new privatisation equity onto the London Stock Exchange over the same period, and the consequent illustration of the market's capacity to absorb large offerings, has played a significant role in London's growth.

The effects of this expansion are only beginning to be felt. The availability of equity finance – with large numbers of individuals now in principal available as investors and with a much larger market – has increased considerably in the countries where mass privatisations have occurred. Companies which would previously have hesitated to undertake large-scale equity issues now begin to see vastly increased opportunities. As a result, projects such as the Anglo–French Channel Tunnel, which might have been impossible to mount a few years ago, now seem thinkable. As privatisation and the development of equity markets spread through Third World countries, the effects could be even more marked. Combined with equity swaps organised by overseas banks intent on reducing their exposure to Third World debt, privatisation could substantially alter the structure of the capital market and the requirement for external debt in Third World countries, and could gradually bring to a halt the spiralling debt–equity ratios which have caused so much trouble for these countries. This aspect of privatisation has begun to be recognised. In a letter to the major national newspaper in Jamaica (*Daily Gleaner* (Kingston), November 1986), the president of the Private Sector Organisation of Jamaica wrote:

> The PSOJ welcomes the Government's speed-up of the divestment process which carries benefits for the public treasury as well as for greater internal economic efficiency. . . These divested entities will now have the ability to secure the required investment funding, consistent with their long-term economic viability. This is likely to enhance the companies' efficiency and the country's development prospects.

Conclusion

Altogether, the reasons for engaging in privatisation – although diffuse and often discovered in the course of the activity rather than known in advance – constitute a powerful and impressive array. The particular aspects of the policy that prove attractive vary from one country to another, but this flexibility has proved to be an advantage rather than a difficulty, making privatisation a welcome opportunity even in countries which might at first have seemed to be hostile territory. The distrust of the state as a manager of enterprise – the feeling that lies at the heart of all the arguments for privatisation – has been complemented by, and indeed legitimised by the capacity of the policy to change the nature of government, to increase pressure for operational efficiency, to reduce fiscal deficits and national debt, to expose subsidies and distortions, to clarify regulation, to increase competition, to involve employees and to enlarge the breadth and depth of capital markets. These features of the policy, mostly developed first in the UK, are now seen as practical advantages by governments around the world, giving the enthusiasts support and weakening the case of the doubters. It is such practical advantages, rather than any fully developed theory, that account for the speed with which the movement has spread. In this respect, the vogue for privatisation is remarkably different from the vogue for nationalisation which preceded it in the 1940s and 1950s. In place of theory, there is a gut feeling and a practical record.

3

ANSWERING THE OPPONENTS

The Main Criticisms

Like any new fashion, privatisation has had its critics. And it is in the UK – the motherland of privatisation – that the art of such criticism has reached its most advanced state. Because of the extent and longevity of the programme, every species of critic has had a chance to develop lines of attack, and to respond to changing circumstances with new forms of opposition. The critics in the UK include, of course, politicians and union leaders. They also include the managers of nationalised industries and state-run services, the environmental lobby, members of the government machine, radical free-marketeers and many other members of the establishment. Perhaps surprisingly, the most famous of all the criticisms was levelled by the former Conservative Prime Minister, Harold Macmillan (Lord Stockton). Accounts of the remarks made by Lord Stockton at a dinner of the Tory Reform Group in London on 8 November 1985 vary in detail. But the general gist is clear. As *The Times* reported the following day:

Lord Stockton said: 'First of all the Georgian silver goes, and then all that nice furniture that used to be in the salon. Then the Canalettos go.' Cable & Wireless, 'a tasty morsel', had been sold off. Profitable parts of the railways and steel industry along with the telephone system had also been sold: 'they were like the two Rembrandts still left'. He said: 'Now we are promised a further sale of anything else that can be scrapped up.' And turning to Mr Walker [the Energy Secretary] he said: 'You cannot sell the coal mines, I am afraid.' He said that the government had got away with the sale of assets on a colossal scale, assets which could never be replaced.

The phrase 'selling the family silver' served to ensure that these points were noted around the world; they now form one of the *loci classici* of debates about the merits of privatisation.

Another, related accusation has been that these 'national assets' are being sold off too cheaply. When the privatisation of British Gas was mooted, Mr John Edmonds, General Secretary of the General Municipal Boilermakers and Associated Trades Union (GMBATU) objected vigorously, saying that gas industry assets were worth £16 billion and might be sold for only £6 billion (*Financial Times*, 25 March 1986). When Vickers Shipbuilding and Engineering was sold to a management–employee consortium, the Labour Party's trade and industry spokesman, Mr Alan Williams, criticised the move saying that it was an abuse of public funds to sell the shipyard for £100 million or less when £200 million of public money had already been invested in it (*Guardian*, 8 March 1986). At the Labour Party Conference of 1985, a prominent member of the Party's National Executive Council, Mr David Blunkett, summed up this line of attack:

In introducing the debate on social ownership and privatisation, I should like to pose to Conference a question that arises in every household; would you dream of selling your furniture, washing machine, freezer and car in order to rent them back at a cost greater than that you paid in the first place? Would you sell your house and then buy back the door to give yourself a stake in the house you originally owned? Would you take a house, improve it and then sell it at the original price that you would have got before you invested in it? Would you do any of these things? Of course you would not, but the Tory government is doing that with our industry, our economy and our nation (*Labour Party Conference Report*, 1985).

In the early days of privatisation these generalised criticisms that something was being improperly 'given away' were matched

53

by technical criticisms of the price levels chosen by the government and its financial advisers. Amersham was said to be 'underpriced', with an immediate premium in the after-market of 46p, and Britoil was said to be 'overpriced', with shares, bought for an initial payment of 100p, exchanging hands on the day of issue for only 81p. The mood changed somewhat after the British Telecom sale, when it became clear that underpricing could be used as a deliberate tool to attract a very large number of small investors, turning this into an aspect of social policy rather than a mere technical mistake. But the critics have not disappeared. David Blunkett, again, was eloquent:

> 50 per cent of British Telecom shares went to institutional shareholders; 20 per cent went abroad; only 25 per cent went to individual shareholders. Three-quarters of a million of those shares were sold in the first few days at a 90 per cent mark-up. . . It is nonsense and we have to expose it as nonsense (*Labour Party Conference Report*, 1985).

Mr J.D. Daly, of the National Association of Local Government Officers, was even more explicit:

> The real worth went into the hands of those readers of the *Financial Times* who were unable to believe their luck when they read in their paper – the *Sporting Life* or the *City Speculator* – that the government has sold British Telecom for a sum of £1,300,000,000 less than its initial stockmarket value. This was the figure established by the real sale of the century, one that took place after the BT flotation, when around £1,000,000,000 worth of shares changed hands for a handsome profit. The government has also sold Amersham International, Associated British Ports, Jaguar, British Aerospace, Cable & Wireless and the state share in British Petroleum – all of them sold, your assets, at knock-down prices. It amounts to a national scandal (*TUC Conference Report*, 1985).

From this accusation that the price of the privatisation has been too low, it is only a short step to the further accusation that the whole process is corrupt; and the critics of the policy have been very willing to take this step. Mr Daly is a case in point:

> Congress, we are dealing with a model form of political corruption. Thatcher is aiming not only to buy votes – that is corrupt – but to do so with public money by financing tax cuts and the issue of free shares to the employees of privatised companies from the sale of our collective assets. That makes it doubly corrupt (*TUC Conference Report*, 1985).

In addition to the informal charge of corruption, there is the more formal charge of illegality. During the sale of the Trustee Savings Bank, a number of legal challenges were mounted to show that the bank was owned by its depositors rather than the government, and that it consequently could not be privatised. These challenges were rejected by a unanimous decision of the House of Lords in July 1986 and it was decided, in effect, that no one owned the bank. TSB Central Board was therefore set up as the solitary shareholder and all proceeds from the sale were paid over by the Board to the company, TSB Group plc. Similar challenges have been contemplated in the case of the water authorities, with the unions reportedly preparing to show that the government does not own the authorities and has no right to privatise them. Warning shots have already been fired by the unions suggesting that the water authorities may be spending money promoting privatisation, in conflict with their terms of reference under the Water Act.

Another contentious issue has been foreign involvement in privatisation. There was opposition even from Conservative MPs, led by the former Prime Minister Mr Edward Heath, when the government attempted to sell two divisions of the British Leyland Motor Company to overseas purchasers. On 8 March 1986, the *Guardian* expressed the feelings of many opponents by saying that privatising car companies in bits might sound fine, but not when it meant putting flourishing and desirable enterprises into US hands. Indeed, the pressure became so great that the government was ultimately forced to abandon the deal, but not before the leader of the National Union of Railwaymen had predicted that privatisation of British Rail workshops would mean them, too, falling into the hands of the dreaded General Motors

(*Daily Telegraph, Guardian, Financial Times*, 20 June 1987). The General Motors case was, however, only the most extreme example of a general tendency. Throughout the privatisation programme, opponents have argued that the policy would, in one way or another, hand over priceless national assets to overseas investors and competitors. In October 1982, the Trades Union Congress's Nationalised Industries Committee wrote to the Secretary of State for Industry during the preparation of the British Telecom sale, claiming that such a sale would abandon the industry in the UK to the huge overseas telecommunications operators searching for export markets. A few years later, Mr David Williams of GMBATU expressed the feelings underlying most if not all of the attacks on foreign involvement: 'Where is the political justification for removing British Gas from public accountability, for taking an asset owned by the people and placing it into the hands of the highest bidder, be they American oil companies, foreign nationals or shady, unnamed speculators' (*Labour Party Conference Report*, 1986).

A further concern voiced by the critics has been that privatisation will somehow prevent the formation of a coherent strategy for the economy. The sale of British Gas provoked a large number of complaints on this score. Mr John Lyons of the Electrical Power Engineers Association said that 'privatisation of British Gas will usher in several years and even several decades of political and economic uncertainty for this industry which cannot possibly be of benefit either to us or the country' (*Financial Times*, 25 March 1986). Mr David Basnett of GMBATU said that the sale should be prevented since British Gas was 'a unique strategic asset' for the nation (*Financial Times, Guardian*, 1 May 1985). Another member of the same union put forward a motion at the Labour Party Conference of 1985, deploring the privatisation of British Gas, on the grounds that it would be: 'sheer madness to place one of the country's energy sources in private hands, and thereby damage any prospect of a future national energy policy' (*Labour Party Conference Report*, 1985). And at the same conference, Mr Ken Cure of the Party's National Executive Council made the case in more general terms:

Only public enterprise can give Britain strategic control in key sectors for the future. Without it we would have no domestically-owned company in sectors such as motor vehicle and aero-engine building, ship building and computers. The NEB established ICL and Inmos to produce British computers and microchips. . . Only public enterprise can create the kind of society that we want – one in which new technologies give people greater control over their lives and in which vital social needs are met as of right, irrespective of income (*Labour Party Conference Report*, 1985).

Another criticism has been that privatisation will threaten service standards, safety, and continuity of supply. This has, indeed, been one of the most consistent lines of attack and is still very much in vogue in the UK. Dire warnings of this sort were made when the privatisation of British Telecom was being discussed in the early 1980s. At that time Mr Alan Tuffin of the Union of Communication Workers prophesied that privatisation would lead to the loss of 77,000 telephone boxes, particularly in rural areas, and he launched a publicity campaign to persuade the public that the danger should be taken seriously (*Financial Times*, *Times* and *Guardian*, 13 April 1983). Four years later, in June 1987, Mr Tuffin issued a similar prophecy about privatisation of the Post Office, saying that it would mean a cut in postal services, again particularly in rural areas (*Guardian*, 1 June 1987). Nor has this view been taken only by the unions. Just two days after Mr Tuffin's latter statement, Sir Ron Dearing, Chairman of the Post Office, argued forcefully against any form of privatisation which involved splitting up the various activities of the Post Office, saying that such a move would inevitably lead to a deterioration of services (*Times*, 3 June 1987). These remarks followed the launching of a campaign by four separate unions, representing both managers and workers in the postal service, who jointly argued that privatisation would mean the cutting of rural post offices, ending of Saturday deliveries and the closure of district sub-post offices.

In the case of British Gas, the limelight was on safety standards. At the Labour Party Conference, the motion put forward by the GMBATU specifically stated that: 'because of the threat to safety standards [this conference] commits the Labour Party to

57

renationalisation of British Gas with compensation being on the basis of proven need only' (*Labour Party Conference Report*, 1985). And at the same conference, an individual delegate made the point even more forcefully:

> If the gas industry is put into private hands, it is not just the Police that will be needed down there with metal detectors looking at what happens. People will be needed down there with gas detectors, because there is no doubt that mains will not be repaired as quickly in private ownership as they were in public ownership. Do we want an industry that is more dangerous and potentially lethal than terrorist bombs, to be in the hands of private contractors in private industry? (*Labour Party Conference Report*, 1985).

Equally strong complaints about standards for the consumer have been made in relation to privatised local government services. A delegate at the 1985 Trades Union Conference stated that: 'Privatisation has been a disaster in the Health Service. The simplistic money-saving measures have created turmoil in hospitals, conflict between groups of staff and the worst public and industrial relations since the start of the Health Service' (*TUC Conference Report*, 1985). A motion passed at the 1985 Labour Party Conference specifically stated that 'privatisation reduces the standard of service to the public' (*Labour Party Conference Report*, 1985) and Mr Blunkett made an eloquent statement about the effect of privatisation on service levels:

> When Wirral District Council . . . went out for tender for its waste collection service, it had a tender . . . the tender would have meant that the sixty men that it intended to employ . . . would have done 27 miles a day at an average of 8.7 miles an hour, just outside the qualifying time for the Olympic marathon [applause]. The firm that got the tender received 600 complaints a day in the first two months of its contract. There have been 1,000 complaints in Wandsworth about the privatised cleansing service (*Labour Party Conference Report*, 1985).

The criticism has also been focused on consumer prices resulting from privatisation. Mr Jeremy Mitchell, Director of the National Consumer Council, commenting on the government's plans for the privatisation of British Gas said, 'gas bills could rise, while the industry piles up massive profits and standards of service drop' and added 'in its present form it offers a worthless prospectus for consumers'. A *Financial Times* report (8 January 1986) stated that:

> In a briefing note for MPs the [NCC] hightlights several weaknesses in the Bill. The price formula takes no account of the eventuality that British Gas may increase prices while at the same time lowering its standards. British Gas could pass the cost of the gas it buys directly on to the consumer. The proposed watchdog, Ofgas, would not have enough power or financial backing to ensure that consumers' interests were properly protected.

A further, long running complaint has been the effect of privatisation on jobs and wages. At the TUC Conference of 1982, a representative of the Post Office Engineering Union moved that:

> Congress records its alarm and total opposition to the policy of this Conservative government to privatise large parts of the National Health Service, local government services and the nationalised industries. Congress opposes all such destructive moves which put profit before service, and threaten the conditions of employment and recognised negotiating procedures of the staff (*TUC Conference Report*, 1982).

Three years later, at the Labour Party Conference of 1985, a motion was adopted which stated that privatisation 'depresses already appallingly low wage rates and conditions of service' (*Labour Party Conference Report*, 1985). In early 1987, the General Secretary of the Transport and General Workers' Union (Britain's largest union) warned that privatisation of the Royal Ordnance Factories would lead to the loss of up to 20 per cent of the factories' jobs (*Financial Times* and *Guardian*, 25 March 1987).

Similar fears were expressed by the unions when Ministry of Defence dockyards were privatised. And the motion adopted two years earlier at the Labour Party Conference stated that the privatisation of British Gas would 'Put at risk 100,000 jobs of those directly or indirectly employed, as the privatised company seeks short-term, higher profits at the expense of long-established, safe and highly technical procedures' (*Labour Party Conference Report*, 1985).

The strongest complaints about conditions of service and jobs have, however, been reserved for the privatisation of local services. A delegate at the Labour Party Conference described the behaviour of private contractors for local services as 'inhuman' and amplified this, stating that: 'The main method by which contractors undercut public services is by basing their tenders on fewer jobs, big cuts in take-home pay and far worse sickness, holiday and pension entitlements' (*Labour Party Conference Report*, 1985). Another delegate went even further:

> Workers in the caring services, school meals, home-help, cleaning are low paid . . . and they have been blackmailed for years into believing that if they took low pay their jobs would be safe. My goodness how wrong they were. Allowing this legislation will mean another quarter of a million workers on the dole (*Labour Party Conference Report*, 1985).

These complaints about the immediate effect of privatisation on the consumer and the worker are matched by fears about the effect that privatisation could have on long-term national patterns of investment. Commenting on the plans to privatise British Gas, a motion adopted by the Labour Party Conference claimed: 'This move will destroy the hope of much-needed investment in other parts of industry through the pre-emption of resources' (*Labour Party Conference Report*, 1985). This is only one variation on the theme. The opponents of privatisation have also argued what might appear at first sight to be the opposite case – namely that the privatised company itself will be unable to match the level of investment provided in the public sector. The Confederation of Shipbuilding and Engineering Unions, for example, made this a central theme of their opposition to the privatisation of Rolls-

Royce, arguing that the company had been a failure in private ownership before and that in private hands it would not be able to continue the research and development programme required for an aero-engine company (*Guardian, Times* and *Daily Telegraph*, 9 June 1986). Nor has this view been restricted to the unions. One Conservative MP in 1986 described the idea of selling off the remainder of the British Leyland Motor Company as 'very short-sighted and, frankly, very foolish' because the firm needed far more public investment before it could fulfil its potential and compete in the European car market (*Scotsman*, 12 November 1986).

All in all, British privatisation has not had an easy ride. It has been attacked from many quarters and on many grounds. But there is nothing unique about the British experience. Many of the complaints that have been made in Britain can be found in other countries. After the privatisation of British Telecom the *Australian Financial Review* (10 January 1986) remarked: 'The main beneficiaries of that exercise were the City of London rather than the "consumer". There are some goods and services . . . which by their very nature are best supplied by the public sector'. In response to the announcement that domestic Australian airport terminals were to be sold off, the same newspaper reported that: 'Opponents of the move fear that selling the terminals now could seriously impede future competition in the airline industry' (2 April 1987). And on 6 April it said: 'The worry is that the sale of terminals may be seen as a quick way to grab some easy money in the context of rationalising government properties rather than part of a well thought out policy of deregulation'.

When the privatisation of Quebecair was announced in Canada, remote communities in northern and eastern Quebec demanded that the Canadian Transport Commission hold hearings into the matter. The mayor of a rural area was one of those who prepared briefs asking the Commission to intervene. One of his aides was quite explicit in his attack: 'We used to have two Quebecair flights per day; now the service has ceased and the Quebecair office has been closed' (*Toronto Globe and Mail*, 14 October 1986).

In France the privatisation programme has been called 'an obstacle course' (*Investor*, 2 June 1986). The magazine *Libération* commented on an interview with privatisation minister, Camille Cabana, that the government was 'caught between a desire for overloaded purses, greed and extreme cautiousness'. And the Lex column in *The Financial Times* (11 May 1986) reported that: 'To make matters worse the trade union movement can be expected to mount a vigorous opposition'. The same paper reported on 29 May 1986 that: 'At the same time the government is almost traumatised by the fear that because of the weak capital structure of many of the groups to be privatised, they could fall prey to takeovers by foreign institutions or predatory French financial interests waiting in the wings'. The sale of Paribas caused much debate and the immediate response of several papers was that 'the privatisation programme is just a giveaway of public assets'. More recently, M. Joxe (parliamentary leader of the Socialists) called privatisation a 'scandal', in which the government's friends were receiving bonuses – and this was echoed by a right-wing critic, M. Barre, who accused the government of establishing a 'political–financial oligarchy'.

Fears about job losses were the main objections to the privatisation of Japan National Railways. The *Far Eastern Economic Review* (23 October 1986) commented:

Much of the opposition to the reform revolves around the massive redundancies. Also, there are fears, particularly in rural areas, that fares will go up drastically and that if this proves inadequate to justify the lines' existence, they would be discontinued. The feeling is that profit should not be the sole criterion for starting or scrapping railway lines which play a major role in bringing together regional communities and their cultures.

As privatisation programmes outside the UK gather momentum and begin to affect industries at the core of the economy, there can be little doubt that every one of the attacks made in Britain will gradually be echoed across the world. Accusations that the government is selling the family silver, giving things away too cheaply, accounting corruptly and illegally, opening the door to foreign involvement, destroying a coherent economic policy, prejudicing safety, jobs, and services for the consumer, and misdirecting investment, will all crop up in one form or another when different industries are sold to different groups under different conditions in different places. Just as the proponents of privatisation operate on a hunch, substantiated by a particular rationale applicable to each particular case, so the opponents of privatisation operate on a feeling that the process is intrinsically wrong and sordid, and they express this feeling in particular objections suited to each particular case.

Dealing with the criticisms

No politician contemplating privatisation could afford to ignore this impressive array of objections. Handling the critics has, indeed, been one of the main preoccupations of governments engaging in privatisations. It has involved a delicate balancing act, particularly in the UK where the objections have been most fully developed. If the programme had not made allowances for the various objections, it would have encountered overwhelming political opposition. Indeed the movement towards privatisation, not only in the UK itself but also – in all probability – in the world as a whole, would never have taken place with anything like its present force. On the other hand, if the Thatcher government had taken every criticism to heart and had attempted to privatise only those entities or services which would not have aroused any serious objections, the programme would never have had a chance to develop into anything significant. The key to the success of the British programme – and therefore probably to the spread of privatisation around the world – has been the combination of agility and determination which the Thatcher government has shown: it has recognised the changing nature of the opposition, and rather than being deterred, it has taken appropriate steps to defeat it. This combination of agility and determination, and the success which has flowed from it, has given heart to other governments across the world. But they have not merely observed the UK experience; rather they have learned from it, and have begun to develop their own methods of dealing with the particular objections that are most important in their own countries.

The range of tactics adopted is almost as great as the range of objections levelled. However, the methods used fall into four broad categories: technical gambits; political courage; side-stepping manoeuvres; and the creation of an interest group. To understand the history of privatisation and the reasons for its success, one has to grasp all four of these elements. Had anyone of them been missing, the programme would almost certainly have faltered and come to a halt.

The perfect example of a technical gambit designed to over-come objections to privatisation is the 'golden' or 'special' share. This technique was first used in the UK but has now been applied in France (under the name of *action spécifique*), Canada and Jamaica, and is under consideration in places as diverse as Turkey, Malaysia and Portugal. The purpose of the technique is to enable the government to block excessive foreign shareholding and other hostile takeovers by retaining a single share with special powers. This, at any rate, is how it has been popularly presented and understood. In practice, it is a little more complicated and ingenious. The block on foreign ownership is not actually achieved through the special share itself, but rather through the Articles of the company to be privatised. For example, the Articles of one privatised company in the UK, British Telecom, as described to prospective investors in the prospectus, state that:

> Where any person has . . . an interest in five percent or more of . . . shares, he must notify the Company. Whether or not such a notification is given, where a person has or appears to the Directors or is deemed to have, an interest in fifteen percent or more of such shares, the Articles also require a disposal to be made so as to reduce the interest of such person below fifteen percent and, in default, for a disposal to be made by the Directors on such terms as they think fit. This requirement applies whether or not other persons also have an interest (even if of less than fifteen percent) in the shares concerned. Until this disposal takes place, the holder is unable to vote.

The precise wording and effect of the blocking Article varies from case to case – sometimes explicitly preventing foreign owners from holding more than the stated percentage of the company's share capital, and at other times preventing any individual shareholder from exceeding a stated percentage. The general pattern, however, is consistent: the block is placed in the rules governing the company's activities, not in the special share itself: this applies in the French, Canadian and Jamaican cases as much as in the UK. The real purpose of the special share is not, therefore, to block excessive holdings but rather to enable the government to prevent any change in the rules governing the company after privatisation. This is achieved by giving the special shareholder a crucial right – namely, a veto over any change in the blocking Article and in the Article that establishes the special share itself.

The two great advantages of this special share mechanism are its simplicity and its flexibility. Instead of having to create an extremely elaborate set of mechanisms, within the rules of the company, to prevent those rules being changed after privatisation, the special share merely provides a special class of shareholder who will always be vigilant and will always have the power to veto such manoeuvres. Moreover, the existence of such an ever-vigilant special shareholder, and the consequent removal of the need for an elaborate daisy-chain of interlocking provisions in the Memorandum and Articles of the company, avoids what can otherwise be an extremely restrictive set of rules, impeding the company in various ways. This point was proved in Jamaica, where – in the first mass privatisation – the special share was avoided on the grounds that it might be misunderstood by investors and be considered an attempt by the government to retain control over the company. As a result, a highly elaborate set of provisions had to be built into the Memorandum and Articles of the privatised company (see Appendix 4).

The special share is a particularly good example of the way in which the British government – and, subsequently, other governments – have used clever corporate finance techniques to solve essentially political problems associated with privatisation. Because of this device, the attacks on foreign involvement in privatisation have never become the major issue that they might otherwise have been. The fear that privatised companies would be taken over by other large groupings has also been kept at bay. Moreover, the special share has been used to overcome other potential criticisms in specific cases – giving the government the right, for example, to ensure that the directors of some privatised firms are not foreign citizens, or enabling the government to prevent sale of strategic assets. And yet, because of the flexibility which the technique gives to the company, there have been few complaints from the managers of the companies being privatised about their freedom from manoeuvre after privatisation. Had these conditions not been met, the privatisation programme could well have floundered on such issues alone, thus illustrating the point that the success or failure of a privatisation programme lies at the interstices of politics and finance – financial mechanisms to achieve political ends without excessive financial disruption.

The special share mechanism also illustrates the extent to which, in the course of dealing with the political objections to privatisation, governments have relied on the technical competence not only of the merchant banks but also other members of the financial community such as company registrars and accountants. This is evident, for example, in the elaborate provisions that have been made for enforcement of the block on large individual share holdings in many of the privatised companies. Article 40 of the British Gas Articles is a case in point, warning that:

(a) For the purpose of these provisions, the expression 'interest' is widely defined . . .

(b) If any person has, or appears to the Directors to have, an interest in shares which carry 15 percent or more of the total votes attaching to the relevant share capital (as defined in section 198(2) of the Companies Act 1985) of the Company or is deemed to have such an interest (in a case where the Directors resolve that they are unable to ascertain the position), the Directors shall give notice to all persons (other than persons referred to in (e) below) who appear to them to have interests in the shares concerned and, if different, to the registered holder(s). The notice will set out the restrictions referred to below and will call for the interest concerned to be reduced to less than 15 percent by disposal of shares within 21 days of the notice being given to the registered holder(s) (or such longer period as the Directors consider reasonable). No transfer of the shares to which the interest relates may then be made except for the purpose of reducing the interest to less than 15 percent.

(c) If such a notice is given and is not complied with in all respects to the satisfaction of the Directors and has not been withdrawn, the Directors shall themselves effect such a disposal on such terms as they may determine, based upon advice obtained by them for the purpose.

(d) A registered holder to whom such a notice has been given is not, until the notice has been withdrawn or complied with to the satisfaction of the Directors, entitled in respect of any of his shares to which the interest concerned relates to attend or vote at any general meeting of the Company or meeting of the holders of voting shares, and those rights will vest in the chairman of any such meeting, who may exercise them entirely at his discretion.

Enforcement of provisions such as these require ingenuity and persistence on the part of those who are responsible for maintaining the share register, and considerable expertise on the part of lawyers and accountants. This, in turn, has had a significant effect on the development of sophistication and expertise in the financial community. The handling of share registers, alone, is now far more developed in countries where mass privatisations have taken place, partly because of the very large numbers of new shareholders that such privatisations have introduced, but partly also because of the controls (like the special share arrangements) which the government has imposed on privatisations in order to meet political criticisms. Sophisticated computerised techniques have been developed in several countries to accommodate the complex manoeuvres now required to maintain the stipulated control over large share registers. In other words, the opponents of privatisation, by stimulating ingenious financial responses to political problems, have in their own way contributed to the development and sophistication of capitalism. This is one of history's minor but amusing ironies.

The special share system is not, however, by any means the only example of a new technique introduced to deal with particular objections to privatisation. The framing of statutes and licences has also been extremely important. When British Telecom was being privatised, and it was argued that rural telephone boxes providing a service to the less affluent members of the

67

public in outlying districts would be cut off, the government responded by building tough rules into the licence granted to British Telecom for its operations. The licence required, for example, that the newly privatised company should preserve a certain number of rural telephone boxes and that it should, if necessary, pay for this service from its own profits. Another technique was adopted to overcome worries about rural bus routes once the National Bus Company was privatised. In this case, the anxiety was contained by introducing, in relevant statutes, a provision for local and central government to offer explicit subsidies, enabling bus operators to maintain services that would not otherwise be profitable. This technique has provided proponents of the National Bus Company privatisation with a strong argument. They confidently predict that the new combination of privatisation, competition and explicit subsidies will preserve more effective rural bus services than the previous nationalised regime.

Statutes and licences have also been used to deal with objections on the grounds of safety. In the legislation governing privatisation of British Gas, for example, explicit provision is made for entry and inspection of premises, examination of gas fittings, disconnection of mechanisms, reconnections, and so on. These regulations complement the general powers and duties to protect consumer safety, which the legislation gives to a newly created Director General of Gas Supply. Similar technniques have also been used to allay environmental objections to privatisation. Fears about the safety of the environment were raised when the privatisation of the water authorities was proposed. Union leaders claimed that it would result in 'the return of cholera days' (*East Anglian Daily Times*, 27 June 1987). The British government first proposed a new national inspectorate, new duties for ministers to assess quality, new protections against pollution and new charges to be levied on those causing pollution to cover the cost of removing it. However, the landowning and farming communities had two great fears about these original privatisation proposals. The first was that privately owned water companies would use their powers over the use of water resources to their own commercial advantage and against the interests of other large users such as farmers, who currently enjoy relatively privileged treatment. The second fear was that there would be a natural tendency among commercial water companies to be harder on the farming community than they were on themselves in their efforts to reduce pollution. The gamekeeper, empowered to stamp out poaching, would himself be a poacher. In response, the government suggested setting up a regulatory body to be called the National Rivers Authority.

The creation of independent regulators has, of course, been the technique consistently employed for another purpose – to control price levels for monopolies once privatised. In addition, it is now slowly becoming apparent that the British government's establishment of independent regulatory bodies such as Ofgas and Oftel – originally designed to control price levels – can act as a safety valve to deal with complaints about service. Recently, there have been increasing complaints about the service levels offered by British Telecom. An opinion poll conducted for the National Consumer Council in March 1987 showed that a large number of those questioned thought that BT's services were poor. There was also harsh criticism of BT's standard of service from the charity Age Concern and the National Communications Union. As a result, the Director General of Telecommunications announced a major investigation into the acceptability of the terms and conditions of the public telecommunications operators, and put forward a series of proposals which could eventually penalise British Telecom financially for failure in service standards.

It should not, however, be thought that the arrangements devised in the UK constitute by any means a complete technical answer to the political objections. There are two areas, in particular, where the French arrangements – clearly derived from a critical evaluation of the British experience – have proved more successful in anticipating and dealing with political difficulties. The first of these techniques is the extremely ingenious decision taken by the French government that all the proceeds of privatisation in France should be devoted to reducing the national debt or increasing the capitalisation of the privatised companies. This move, made right at the start of the privatisation programme, has dealt effectively with all the attacks that would otherwise undoubtedly have arisen from commentators claiming that the

French government was 'selling the family silver'. If the funds raised from privatisation are put firmly back into the capital account, either reducing the stock of national debt (and hence in effect increasing the 'net book value' of the French state) or being returned to the company being privatised (hence actually increasing the company's 'net book value'), there can be absolutely no accusation that the process is turning capital into spending or that it is in any sense diminishing the stock of national assets. Moreover, this policy has a serious economic rationale. By ensuring that the proceeds are devoted to the capital account, the French government has prevented itself from using privatisation as a means of masking increased public expenditure; the policy is therefore a self-constraining measure, of which any treasury or finance ministry would be proud.

The second ingenious technique introduced in France at the beginning of the process was the establishment of an independent committee, charged with the duty of setting a minimum price for each privatisation. This had the effect of reducing fears about 'knock-down prices', which would otherwise undoubtedly have caused as much difficulty in France as they have in the UK. Whether, in practice, the minimum price set by the committee will ever have been higher than the price which would otherwise have been recommended by investment banks and adopted by the government is a matter for speculation: it seems likely that the practical effect of the committee may be extremely limited. However, from the point of view of political objections, the move is a master-stroke. It prevents any accusation that the government is manipulating prices for political purposes and thereby minimises the risk of accusations of 'corruption'. If the privatisation programme had begun in France and had been copied in the UK, rather than vice versa, it seems altogether possible that the UK would have learnt the same lesson and would have adopted the same technique.

Techniques alone are not, however, sufficient to deal with the political arguments. Very considerable political courage may also be necessary. Some of the arguments made against privatisation cannot be dealt with by introducing changes in the rules of the companies being privatised or in the legislation governing the privatisation. They have to be met head-on by a government willing to argue the contrary. The only way of countering 'the strategic industry' argument, for example, is to argue explicitly that the existence of nationalised industries does not increase the chances of coherent economic development, and that the government is capable of running an economic policy without becoming involved in the economy as an owner of industries. Nor are words and arguments by themselves sufficient: privatisation requires another form of political courage – the will to take action. There are always commentators saying that 'the time is not yet right' for any particular privatisation. It will be argued either that the business would be more profitable if left longer, or that the contingent liabilities of the company make a later date preferable, or that the market needs further development, or any number of other such points. If the governments which have engaged in privatisation had heeded such arguments, their programmes would never have begun. The case of the UK illustrates this perfectly. Contrary to the forecasts made in the early 1980s, British Leyland's nationalised four-wheel drive business went from profit into loss, became cash-hungry, lost market shares to overseas competition and was less saleable than before. Again contrary to the forecasts, the microchip company, Inmos, plunged into loss. The difference was that, in the case of Inmos, the government had ignored forecasts and had privatised while the going was good, leaving Thorn EMI, the purchasers of the businesses, to take the losses; in the case of British Leyland's four-wheel drive business the forecasts were heeded, privatisation was delayed and the taxpayer has paid.

Perhaps the biggest example of political courage has been in relation to jobs in nationalised industries. The arguments of the critics – that privatisation would entail massive job losses – would have seemed to be thoroughly justified if governments had attempted to privatise companies while they were dramatically overstaffed and had left the private sector to do the hard work of reducing manning levels. In practice, therefore, governments which have been serious about privatising those industries which suffer from significant over-manning have had to take the step of reducing the number of jobs while the industry remained in public hands. In New Zealand, the socialist government has exhibited such courage to an extreme extent, making deep cuts in the workforce of industries such as the coal mines as part of the 'corporatisation' process, so that the companies will be able to prosper once they are reliant on private sector funding. The Thatcher government in the UK has exhibited similar courage in industries such as steel, where the workforce was reduced by 35 per cent between 1981 and 1983, beginning a turnaround of the profitability of that industry and setting it on a road which may well lead to eventual privatisation.

However, discretion can in some cases be the better part of the valour required for privatisation. Ingenious techniques and courage to take unpopular decisions have to be matched by clever decision-making at crucial moments. An interesting example of this point is the treatment of Leyland Trucks by the UK government. Talk of handing this ailing division over to General Motors provoked intense hostility, and it looked as though closure might prove the only option. But a subtle understanding of the difference in popular perception between US motor giants and their smaller European counterparts proved the vital ingredient. In 1986, a merger between Leyland Trucks and DAF of the Netherlands took the division firmly into the private sector with hardly a whisper of discontent in Britain. What had once seemed a hostile intrusion into British business life by an American Big Brother now seemed like a friendly rescue by a European ally. It is in understanding such differences and in making use of them that a government creates the initiative and disarms its critics.

It is, however, extremely doubtful whether the UK programme – and hence the general movement towards privatisation across the world – would have been sustainable on the basis of techniques, courage and dexterity. Even together, these would almost certainly not have provided the impetus for a positive privatisation programme (as distinct from the denationalisations of the 1960s and 1970s). Overwhelmingly the most important element in making privatisation a positive political success has been the far more fundamental step of creating a great interest group in its favour. By bringing vast numbers of employees and small investors into the programme – by making them shareholders of the privatised companies, and thereby giving them a stake in the companies and the programme itself – the British government, and subsequently other governments, have changed the political landscape. Instead of employees feeling that privatisation is being carried out over their heads, they have been brought into the action and have been made to feel that it is an opportunity for them. That, in the end, has been the effective response to union criticisms and to the attempts by unions to create employee dissatisfaction. For the small man, too, privatisation has come to be seen as an opportunity. There are now, perhaps, 15 million people in England and France alone with a direct stake in privatisation. Instead of the fat cats reaching into the larder, these governments have taken the lead in furthering programmes of mass privatisation which explicitly favour the small investor, making him – and in his person millions of voters – sceptical about all the arguments levelled by the critics. Indeed, the critics themselves have gone into retreat – with figures such as the British Labour Party's trade and industry spokesman admitting that 'the idea of owning shares is catching on and, as socialists, we should support it as one means of taking power from the hands of a few and spreading it more widely' (*Financial Times*, 26 September 1987). Such governments have, in other words, seized the initiative by creating an overwhelming lobby of advocates. The way in which that lobby has been created, the slow faltering beginning, gradually gathering pace and momentum, is the real story of the privatisation phenomenon.

4

BRINGING ABOUT THE PHENOMENON

How has privatisation been achieved in so many countries across the world? How have governments built up interest groups capable of overwhelming the critics and providing a continuous momentum for the policy?

Both of these questions can be answered, but the answers to them are different. It is only in a few countries that sustained programmes of mass privatisation, capable of establishing a really powerful interest group, have been undertaken. In most parts of the world, privatisation has – so far – a more restricted meaning. It typically takes one of three forms: contracting-out of government services, deregulation of activities previously dominated by the public sector, and sales of public assets to existent private sector companies (commonly referred to as 'trade sales'). By themselves, these methods do not have the power to achieve fundamental and lasting shifts in the balance between public and private sectors. Nor are they sufficient to capture the political limelight either within the countries where they are employed or internationally. Nevertheless, these are important and powerful tools, each of which is particularly suited to the privatisation of a particular aspect of the public sector: contracting-out for public services, deregulation for statutory monopolies, and trade sales for companies in poor financial condition.

Contracting-Out

One of the most remarkable features of the British privatisation programme is that, although its main focus has been on spectacular and massive offerings, it has by no means neglected these other methods of achieving privatisation. Contracting-out is no exception. Since 1979 local government in the UK – under pressure from central government – has made extensive use of this form of privatisation for the delivery of local services and has made considerable savings as a result (see p.35).

Contracting-out has in fact proved to be an indispensable tool for privatising local government services. Full privatisation, involving sale of public sector assets and complete transfer of responsibility to the private sector, virtually depends on the possibility of the private sector levying charges. Normal trading companies engaged in manufacturing are straightforward examples: they can be sold entirely to the private sector because they can survive through profits made out of sales. In the case of local services, such as garbage collection and street cleaning, British local authorities do not normally levy charges, and there would be considerable resistance from local users if charges were levied following privatisation. Local authorities which wish to privatise services are therefore virtually compelled to find another means of doing so. Contracting-out of the services to private operators provides the ideal means, since the local authority retains financial responsibility, paying the operators a fee out of tax revenues for the provision of the service and thereby avoiding the need for direct charging of the customer.

To establish a regime under which relative levels of efficiency could be assessed, British local authorities have typically set up a competitive tendering process in three stages. The first of these is the preliminary announcement. To start the process, a local authority announces that it is contemplating the contracting-out of a given range of services; a broad description of these services is provided, usually in relevant trade journals. Prospective contractors are invited to submit general descriptions of their firms, their financial condition, their previous experience of similar work and their capacity to take on such work in the future.

The second stage is the invitation to tender. Once the local authority receives responses to the preliminary announcement, serious firms are selected and are invited to tender competitively for the work in question. The local authority sends the contractors a formal invitation to tender and a formal specification document. The specification typically includes the amount of work to be done, the method of pricing (whether it be a schedule of rates per unit or fixed price) and other relevant details.

The final stage is the selection of contractors. When the local authority has received responses to its formal tender documents, a judgement is made on the basis of the prices offered by competitors and their previous track records. A legal contract is agreed with the winning contractor, containing appropriate default and performance bond clauses.

A good example of this process is provided by the London Borough of Wandsworth, which has been a leader in contracting out many different services. The methods employed by this local authority to promote the chances of high service levels and low costs in the case of contracted-out refuse collection are comprehensive and instructive. The specification document asked tenderers to quote a price simply for collection of a given number of bins and bin-equivalents, but an elaborate mechanism was constructed to deal with cyclical changes in levels of refuse: changes of more than 10 per cent in the number of bins collected over a specified period automatically triggered a pro rata escalation or reduction of the total contracting price. All contractors were forced to conform to routes specified by local authorities, which were linked with routes for street cleaning, and were phased to ensure that streets were cleaned after refuse had been collected. This ensured that street-cleaning and refuse could both be contracted out with no danger of disrupting the local authority's careful co-ordination of the two services. Further conditions were included to prevent contractors from operating during anti-social hours or engaging in anti-social activities (such as banging gates). In addition, a complaints mechanism was built into the final contract, ensuring that failure to collect rubbish by a specified time of the day would lead to reductions in payments made by the local authority to the contractor.

Despite such elaborate precautions, British contracting-out has encountered two serious problems – one technical, the other

76

practical. The technical problem centres on the design of the tendering specification and the accompanying contract. It has been difficult to find an appropriate period over which to run the contract – contracts of under five years have proved unattractive to the private sector, while contracts of more than three years have caused problems for local politicians who wish to retain flexibility and control. It has also been difficult to identify a suitable unit of work in some services. It has also not been easy to establish appropriate pricing mechanisms, which allow for genuine changes such as inflation or alterations in the nature of the work being undertaken, and yet provide sufficient constancy for the local authority to achieve proper cost control.

The practical problem has been the difficulty of enforcing service standards. In the first six months of the contracting-out of Wandsworth's street cleaning, the firm to whom the service had been contracted was penalised to the tune of £7,665 (*Financial Times*, 24 September 1982) for not meeting the required standards. The same company was also given the contract for gardening services and a penalty of £45,000 was exacted for poor performance (*Sunday Times*, 31 July 1983). Low standards were blamed on a lack of planning, although there were also accusations of sabotage (*Investors Chronicle*, 5 August 1983). Other local authorities have also suffered from inadequate inspection when refuse collection and school-cleaning have been contracted out, and the National Health Service has suffered extensive criticism as a result of its inadequate inspection of service standards when hospital cleaning and catering have been contracted out in some areas.

Despite these problems, however, contracting-out in Britain has generally been a success – as the case of Wandsworth illustrates. With savings of up to 50 per cent on many services, the result of contracting-out has been, to quote *The Sunday Times* (10 August 1986), that 'on almost every count, Wandsworth provides a better service than Lambeth [the neighbouring borough] – yet it still charges its residents half the rates [local taxes] collected in Lambeth'. Britain is not, however, by any means the only country to have engaged in the contracting-out of public services. It is not even the leader in the field. That mantle falls definitely on the USA.

A prime case in the USA has been urban public transport. With increasing car ownership, private sector bus operators began to make losses from the 1940s onwards, and an increasing share of the market was taken into public ownership. In 1940, some 20 per cent of urban bus routes were in the public sector; by the 1980s the figures had risen to over 80 per cent. Costs in real terms rose almost as fast as the spread of public ownership: according to one estimate, inflation-adjusted costs rose by just under 17 per cent between 1940 and 1955 and by over 50 per cent between 1970 and 1983. A system of competitive tendering and contracting-out has been used by American cities to achieve private sector efficiency and concomitant cost savings, while continuing the public subsidies without which urban public transport would undoubtedly have collapsed. Various surveys conducted by the American Bus Association and others indicate that this policy has succeeded, bringing about cost savings ranging between 10 and 60 per cent, with an average of around 30 per cent. A particularly impressive example is San Diego Transit, where the contracting-out of some services seems to have had a dramatic effect on the remaining public sector services:

Before competitive contracting, costs at the public monopoly, San Diego Transit, had increased at a rate similar to that of other California public transport monopolies. However, the competitive market induced cost control at San Diego Transit. From 1979 to 1984 real public transport costs in California rose 24 per cent while real costs at San Diego Transit increased less than 2 per cent. And system-wide, including both public and competitive operations, real costs declined 3 per cent. By 1984, the comparative improvement in cost performance had saved the San Diego area more than $40 million (Wendell Cox, 'Privatisation in the Public Services', paper presented to the Fraser Institute Privatisation Conference, Vancouver, 1987).

Public transport is by no means the only service which has been contracted out in the United States. As in Britain, refuse collection and street-cleaning have frequently been privatised in this way, as have road maintenance, school-cleaning and catering and

78

institutional care for the elderly. Indeed, even in prisons, over-crowding and unsatisfactory conditions, combined with a Supreme Court ruling that inmates could sue for remedies against poor confinement conditions, led the authorities to contract out management. As a result, organisations such as the Corrections Corporation of America now manage large numbers of contracted-out prisons. Interestingly, although the contracts sometimes include the construction of a prison, the contractor is normally paid only for services performed at a per diem rate per inmate, with construction costs added to the running costs and amortised over the duration of the contract.

Contracting-out has also been used for many years as a tool for privatising local services in Canada: in fact, transport services in British Columbia were being contracted out before this method was used in the USA and UK. Refuse collection, construction and maintenance, protection of people and property, libraries and elements of local administration are also frequently contracted out. One estimate suggests that, as early as 1980, some 40 per cent of domestic refuse collection was contracted out in Canadian municipalities, with a cost saving of more than 25 per cent compared with cases in which municipal authorities took on the jobs themselves, and with an average productivity improvement of roughly 100 per cent; in one municipality, the costs of refuse collection per house appear to have dropped by roughly 40 per cent when this service was contracted out in 1983 (James McDavid, 'Privatisation in Local Governments in Canada', paper presented to the Fraser Institute Privatisation Conference, Vancouver, 1987).

The methods used for achieving contracting-out in the USA and Canada appear to have been very similar to those used in the UK. Competitive tender arrangements have been set up, selections made and contracts awarded. As in the UK, problems have centred on enforcing high standards of service when designing contracts so that there is sufficient flexibility and sufficiently robust cost control. Perhaps the only major difference between the North American programmes and that of the UK has been that federal governments in North America have not (unlike the British central government) attempted to impose competitive tendering and contracting-out on local authorities which would otherwise have been reluctant to adopt such schemes; as a consequence, there has been no friction between central and local government similar to that generated in the UK.

Japan, too, has had a major contracting-out programme for local services. Indeed, the contracting-out of a wide range of services has been the norm in Japanese cities for many years. Activities such as office-cleaning and architectural design are contracted out in some 80 per cent of Japanese cities, while roughly 50 per cent or more of other forms of cleaning, security, microfilming, some forms of computing, waste and refuse collection, fee collection, meter-reading, surveying and publications are contracted out. Several interesting features distinguish the Japanese experience from that of the UK and North America. Competitive tendering is less common, with many contracts being awarded on the basis of negotiations with a single firm. Local individuals and local citizens' groups are frequently employed on a contract basis, and indeed dominate in certain areas such as home services for the disabled and meter-reading. A large number of contracts are awarded on a lump-sum basis (that is, with no specific allowance for the number of tasks performed). And monitoring of performance is more developed than in the UK or USA, with special management improvement commissions and efficiency sections set up in some cities. Perhaps because of these features, the emphasis has been on improvements in quality of service rather than on cost cutting, with nearly 50 per cent of contracting cities reporting that they have made improvements in the quality of service (J.T. Marlin, *Privatisation of Local Government Activities: Lessons from Japan*, AIMS, New York, 1982).

Contracting-out is not, however, restricted to local services or, indeed, to services as a whole. It has also been used as a method of achieving privatisation of industrial activities in a large number of countries. To name just a few instances: a rubber plant and sugar mill have been contracted out to the private sector in Cameroon; the management of Air Zaire has been contracted out to a foreign airline; wells and irrigation projects have been contracted out in Pakistan; and public sector hotels have been leased to private sector operators in numerous countries including Sierra Leone, Jamaica, Grenada and Tunisia.

A particularly interesting form of contracting-out is the use of the private sector to undertake major public construction projects that would previously have been undertaken by the public sector. This has typically involved private sector contractors coming forward with a complete package involving construction, financing and operation of a major item under a concession or contract with the government which often takes the form of a lease, returning the asset to the public sector once the private sector investors have received adequate returns. Examples of this form of contracting-out in the UK include the Dartford Tunnel, the London Docklands Light Railway and the construction of a lignite-fired power station in Northern Ireland. Examples in other countries include major power stations in Turkey and the construction of a new tunnel under Sydney Harbour.

The issues which arise in connection with such projects are complex and difficult. Governments have aimed to ensure that risks are genuinely transferred to the private sector – sensibly enough, since this is the only reason for seeking private sector financing, which will almost inevitably involve a higher cost of capital than government funds. But achievement of such a transfer of risk depends on the details of the lease, concession or contract between the government and the private sector. If, for example, a tunnel or bridge is being financed and constructed by the private sector, the private investors will typically seek their returns through a concession over tolls. If this concession is for a fixed period at a genuinely fixed cost, both investors and contractors bear a significant risk that the returns on the capital invested, once allowance is made for the actual construction costs, will be unattractive. However, if the concession allows the private sector investors to increase the concession period or the level of toll when construction turns out to cost more than was anticipated, the risks will not really be borne by the private sector, but will rather accrue to the consumer. Since the sums involved can be very large – rising to $1 billion or more – considerable ingenuity may be exercised by the private sector in attempting to avoid genuine risk, making the negotiation of the lease, concession and contract terms enormously demanding for the bureaucracy and its advisers. This use of the private sector to carry the burden of what would otherwise be major public sector projects is therefore

81

the most challenging as well as the most potentially far-reaching of the forms of contracting-out.

The history of the Sydney Harbour Tunnel provides a good example of the scale of this sort of project. Sydney Harbour Bridge, one of the miracles of modern engineering, was a massive public sector project. However, the bridge did not prove sufficient to handle Sydney's growing traffic, and throughout the 1980s the New South Wales government attempted to find some means of building a new structure. A number of proposals were put up, including one to build a second bridge, which was withdrawn following strong protests from those living in the residential areas that would have been affected. In 1986, a major private sector consortium of bankers and engineering companies put up a A$350 million project to establish twin two-lane tunnels under the harbour, funded through toll revenue – with the revenues accruing to the private sector consortium for 15 years, after which the tunnel would revert to government ownership. After a feasibility study, the government decided to alter the route and opted for a rather more expensive version, costing some A$435 million with a concession period of 30 years and indexed tolls. A good measure of the complexity of the operation is the fact that, although there was no formal competitive tender for the project, the private consortium was said to have spent some A$300,000 on designing the original proposal in addition to A$2 million on the feasibility study.

Deregulation

Another, quite different, technique for bringing the private sector into areas where previously only the public sector dared to tread is deregulation. In principal, this technique is the easiest of all: as the name implies, the government merely removes regulations which previously prevented the private sector from competing with a nationalised monopoly. In practice, the process is more complicated and the name is misleading: 'deregulation' is often a matter not merely of removing regulations that previously existed, but also of constructing new regulations to change the competitive environment.

This technique has been used in a large number of countries.

In 1985, the Japanese government removed Nippon Telephone and Telegraph's monopoly and, in particular, opened up two new areas for private sector competitors: leased lines and 'value-added' information services. The move was intended to introduce both new technology and overseas investment into Japanese telecommunications – and the opportunities that it offered were immediately taken up by a joint venture between Japanese private sector companies and AT&T, offering a new value-added network. A total of four new common carriers started leased circuit services, charging rates some 20 per cent lower than those of NTT. Another rapidly expanding business is that of portable electronic paging: as a result of deregulation, a stream of new companies have been attracted to this field and officials in Japan expect 20–30 new companies to be established in the next year or two (*JIJI Press*, 14 April 1987).

In a similar review, the Canadian government, during 1985, announced proposals to deregulate transport, particularly the airline industry. The idea was to reach new agreements with the USA, increasing the number of routes which could be travelled by Canadian airlines, and then to allow private sector airlines to fly these routes so as to decrease Canada's dependence on the public sector carrier, Air Canada. The government announced, in addition, that all domestic air services would be open to private sector operators 'fit, willing and able' to run such services. To make this deregulation effective, the government announced that Crown corporations such as Air Canada would be 'discouraged' from engaging in predatory pricing – an interesting example of new regulation being used as a means of achieving deregulation. Despite this, there have been accusations of cartels being formed to negate the effects of deregulation – leading to enquiries by a Canadian government committee, and calls for the break up of Air Canada which have been strongly resisted by the airline itself. Some of the smaller airlines, whom deregulation was meant to benefit, have also suffered as larger airlines began to pick off passengers by charging lower fares. However, there have been new private sector entrants to the sector, including commuter lines such as Air Atlantic, achieving a measure of privatisation through deregulation.

In the Netherlands, an even more interesting development has taken place. Using deregulation as a means of introducing privatisation by private (rather than government) action, the Dutch Consumer Association, the Consumentenbond, took the government to court in 1986, and argued that the nationalised monopoly of telephone-equipment sales should be abolished for the sake of the consumer. The Consumer Association claimed that the monopoly should be abolished quickly, since cheaper and more modern equipment would be available to consumers if private firms could enter the market. Moreover, this argument worked. The government capitulated, and the Dutch telecommunications market is to be opened up to the private sector in 1989, once appropriate legislation has passed through parliament. The nationalised post and telecommunications agency is to be 'corporatised', becoming an ordinary company, with 100 per cent of its shares held (for the moment) by the government; the supply of terminal equipment is to be deregulated; and the provision of value-added services is to be liberalised.

In a rather more conventional mould, the Spanish government announced in 1986 that it would be introducing a bill to break the state TV monopoly and to establish rules for three new independent channels. The plan was to introduce a new independent regulatory authority, which would supervise renewable contracts for private competitors and ensure that the state transmission network gave adequate access to private operators – another case of new regulation forming part of 'deregulation'.

Another example of the extent to which pro-competitive regulation may be required in order to make a reality of deregulation comes from the electricity supply industry in Britain. In 1983 the British government brought forward an Energy Act which explicitly provided for private sector generators and suppliers to compete with the nationalised Central Electricity Generating Board (CEGB) in the provision of electricity. The Act is quite unequivocal. It states that:

Where a private generator or supplier requests an Electricity Board:
(a) to give and continue to give a supply of electricity to premises where he generates electricity or from which he supplies electricity to others, or

(b) to purchase electricity generated by him, or

(c) to permit him to use the board's transmission and distribution system for the purpose of giving a supply of electricity to any premises,

the Board shall offer to comply with the request unless on technical grounds it would not be reasonably practicable to do so.

In theory, therefore, the generation and supply of electricity in the UK has been 'deregulated' since 1983. However, this is illusion rather than reality. In practice, the Act has done little to create competition for the CEGB from the private sector. This is probably because it also states that: 'Every offer under this section shall include such reasonable terms and conditions as the Board may consider necessary to secure that the control by Electricity Boards of the operation of the electricity supply system is not harmed'. In addition, the Act states that:

The principles on which tariffs are fixed and prices proposed by an Electricity Board in accordance with this section shall include the principle that a purchase . . . should be on terms which:

(a) will not increase the prices payable by customers for electricity supplied to them by the Board, and

(b) will reflect the costs that would have been incurred by the Board but for the purchase.

The effect of these provisions has been to enshrine features of nationalised-industry pricing arrangements which make it highly unattractive for private generators to supply electricity. As a result, the detailed provisions in the Act to ensure that fair competition can be conducted have proved largely ineffectual. Far more stringent, pro-competitive regulation over tariffs and the general structure of pricing in the industry would have been required to introduce real private sector competition in the supply of large new power stations. Indeed, an awareness of this fact has been one of the prime considerations for the government when deciding on a new structure for the industry in preparation for full-scale privatisation.

Trade Sales

A more prosaic, but at least equally common, form of privatisation is the sale of an individual company or asset by the state to an already existent private sector company. Such sales have occurred in a large number of countries including Cameroon, Senegal and Togo in Africa; Bangladesh, Malaysia, Pakistan and Sri Lanka in Asia; Bolivia, Chile, Costa Rica, Honduras, Jamaica, Mexico and Peru in Central and South America; Canada and the United States in North America; and West Germany, Italy, Turkey and the UK in Europe. Typically, such sales have been used by governments to privatise relatively discrete and small-scale units – industrial plants, individual factories and mills of various types. They have also been used to privatise small and medium-sized companies, particularly in South America where it has been by far the most popular form of privatisation.

The advantages of a trade sale are legion. Where a nationalised company or asset is sold by a government to an established private sector company, the transaction involves two knowledgeable parties which can negotiate with one another on relatively equal terms. The government may, of course, wish to conduct a competitive tender to extract the highest price from private sector bidders, but there is no need to worry about formal prospectuses or about misleading those small investors who have neither the time nor the skill to investigate fully what they are buying. Instead, the government can rely on the self-interest of the private sector company to investigate in full the nature of the asset and the liabilities attaching to it. Because the negotiation is conducted between professionals, it can be quick; it can (at least in theory) be conducted in confidence, without any publicity until the deal is complete; and a fair price can be negotiated, avoiding any accusation of an immediate premium or 'selling the silver short'.

This form of sale is particularly suitable for a company whose performance and balance sheet are poor. Unlike small private investors in a public offer, an established private sector company advised by experts can assess risks and can identify opportunities for improving performance through financial restructuring. Moreover, a private sector company can often identify synergies with its own current business, which will make it willing to pay a

86

higher price for a poorly performing nationalised asset or company than would be paid by any individual or institutional investor. This, indeed, explains why trade sales have been such a recurrent feature of South American privatisation – since South American governments have typically seen privatisation as primarily a means of divesting nationalised assets which have not been performing well. Often, the choice has been liquidation or trade sale, since no investor apart from another private sector would have been willing to buy many of the assets on offer.

When conducting a trade sale, governments typically attempt to create interest among prospective purchasers by preparing a fairly full information memorandum, which contains much the same background information about the company as would normally be provided in a prospectus for a public offer. One South American memorandum, for example, contains a detailed analysis of the background and present structure of the company, its commercial position, operations, staffing, subsidiaries, legal position and accounts. Another, European, memorandum is extremely similar, containing a history of the company, a description of its corporate structure, a detailed description of each of its divisions, an analysis of its current projects and future products, a description of its research and development programme, an outline of its suppliers, competitive position, relationship with the sponsoring ministry, management, employees, industrial relations, pension schemes, redundancy terms, insurance arrangements, accounting and management information schemes, net assets, trading record and future plans for financial reconstruction. Since such documents are prepared by professionals for professionals, there is no need for polished prose and simplifications. On the contrary, the emphasis is on getting the facts straight so that sensible price negotiations can be started.

Trade sales are not, however, in every case instigated by the government. On the contrary, there have been numerous cases of companies in the private sector making bids on their own initiative for government assets once a privatisation programme is under way. Indeed, governments which have set up active privatisation programmes have frequently found themselves besieged by bidders of this type. Often, the bidders will employ financial advisers of their own and make specific and ingenious proposals.

A bid document prepared by such a bidder will typically include a description of the formal terms of the bid, a record of informal discussions that the bidder has held with the government and the nationalised company for which the bid is being made, a summary of the bidder's financial position and proof – in the form of underwriting or otherwise – that the private sector company could carry the bid into action if accepted by the government. In addition, some rather impudent bidders will provide the government with draft contracts and other material necessary to complete the transaction in a hurry. Sometimes inducements to accept the bid are also offered in the form of specially designed packages for employees and an offer to take some other particularly unpromising item off the government's books at the same time.

Governments in receipt of such bids have to be wary. In practice, the private sector company making the bid probably knows a great deal more than the civil servants about the financial prospects and real value of the nationalised asset for which it is bidding. This is particularly true in the case of small nationalised assets which will not have come to the attention of the ministry except at moments of emergency. Ministers and officials can all too easily slide into agreeing what appears at first sight to be an attractive sale to a particular bidder; they do so at the risk of severe criticism from other potential bidders who may well be aware that the sale has been conducted at a knock-down price – or who may simply have an interest in pretending that this was the case if they have been effectively excluded from the bidding process. There has consequently been an increasing tendency in several countries, both in Europe and South America, to insist on a formal tendering process even where a privatisation has been promoted by a bidder rather than by a government itself.

Crossing the Great Divide

Contracting-out, deregulation and trade sales are serious and important forms of privatisation but they suffer from two overwhelming disadvantages. First, they are defeated by scale: none of these methods can be used to transfer massive nationalised industries in one fell swoop to the private sector. The core activities of such large nationalised industries cannot be contracted out, because there are no contractors with a sufficient asset base to take on the work that they do; they cannot be edged out by private sector competitors, through deregulation, because they are important employers and wealth-creators in their own right, needing to be sustained and improved, not merely replaced; and they cannot be sold to an existing private sector company since there is typically no private sector company big enough to absorb them.

Second, these methods create only a limited interest in favour of privatisation. True, contracting-out makes the private sector contractors and the taxpayers whose bills are reduced into friends of privatisation; deregulation gives the private sector competitors who enter the market and the customers who benefit from lower prices an interest in continued liberalism; and trade sales give the private sector acquirers reasons for opposing nationalisation; but none of these are serious interest groups, capable of making or breaking a government or political party. It is too easy for the opponents of privatisation to appeal to the unions and to the 'public interest' when seeking to renationalise activities being conducted by private sector companies as a result of contracting-out, deregulation or trade sales.

The creation of a significant interest group involves an act of political will which carries a government far beyond these methods of privatisation, into an area of high risk, where every mistake will receive full public attention, and where the sheer complexity of the operation is sufficient to deter faint hearts. It is by making this act of political will and by accepting the political risks inherent in it that Mrs Thatcher has been able to achieve such a marked impact on the British political scene and on the prospects for privatisation across the world. Using two high-profile techniques – the management–employee buyout and the public offer – she has brought into play two vital interest groups as allies of privatisation: employees and small investors.

Interestingly, a precedent for this form of risk-taking was set by a policy which is unique to the UK and which has had a profound impact on the social structures – the sale of council houses to their tenants. Public housing in the UK reached enormous proportions in the late 1970s, occupying some 20 per cent of the total housing market. When the Thatcher government first suggested the sale of these council houses to their tenants, the policy was regarded as idealistic but impractical by supporters of the government and as profligate and irresponsible by the government's opponents. Some six years later, with approximately 1 million council houses privatised, and with new policies mooted to privatise a further substantial chunk of the public housing stock, the political climate has changed significantly. Some 2 million individuals now have a direct vested interest in this form of privatisation, which is unreservedly accepted by the government's supporters and only mutely criticised by the opposition.

This remarkable experiment in privatisation carried the Thatcher regime across the great divide between mere attempts to reduce the public sector and a much bolder, positive policy of promoting the private sector. If an interest group with enormous political power could be built up by the privatisation of property, it began to seem altogether probable that something of the same sort could be done by privatising companies. The realisation of that fact has been the decisive feature in altering the nature of privatisation, drawing governments towards management–employee buyouts and public offers.

Management–Employee Buyouts

Management–employee buyouts have formed a surprisingly large part of the British privatisation programme. The first major example was the National Freight Corporation, sold to management and employees in February 1982 while the privatisation programme was still in its infancy. Since then, there have been similar buyouts of four of the British Shipbuilders warship yards; over 20 National Bus Company subsidiaries covering large areas of England and Wales; several major subsidiaries of British Leyland including Unipart and Leyland Bus; and Hoverspeed, a subsidiary of British Rail.

The history of these buyouts is interesting. It has involved very considerable risks on the part not only of the government – which has frequently given explicit preference to management–employee consortia, even where a competing bid from a private sector company might have been the safer option – but also for the management and employees themselves, who have frequently borrowed considerable sums of money. An example of both forms of risk is provided by the management–employee buyouts of the Vickers warship yards. The management had to form a consortium to make the bid and had to find some £60 million in immediate payment, with an additional £40 million to be paid from anticipated profits in 1992–3. Since the managers were unable to raise all the necessary cash themselves, they offered 35 million £1 ordinary shares and £40 million of loan stock to the employees, to residents in the area around the shipyards and institutional investors. Although at the time the yards were losing money, and although almost £90 million of debt to British Shipbuilders had to be written off, the consortium succeeded in attracting a merchant bank and three insurance companies as initial stakeholders, purchasing on their own, or on others' behalf, some 33 per cent of the shares. Employees were given interest-free loans enabling them to buy up to 500 shares each, with 150 free shares for anyone buying 500 shares or more. Shares sold to employees and the local community were offered in special offices set up in the shipyards and were widely taken up. Eighty-three per cent of the employees bought 22 per cent of the total company including the free shares. Negotiations with the government were by no means simple. Difficult issues concerning future Ministry of Defence work for the yards had to be settled, particularly as the yards were responsible for the construction of the Trident nuclear submarine. Considerable financial restructuring had to occur, since the subsidiary Cammel Laird yard had been troubled by almost continuous labour difficulties and had suffered substantial losses. When the bids came in, the management–employee consortium's price was not the highest. Nevertheless, the government took – publicly – a decision to favour the consortium in order to spread employee ownership.

The history of the National Freight Corporation is equally interesting. Although National Freight is Britain's largest road-freight business, when the Thatcher government came to power, it had a considerable history of poor performance. In the late 1960s, it was making losses equal to about 80 per cent of its turnover and was vastly overmanned; between the end of the

1960s and 1979, the workforce had been trimmed considerably, new management had been brought in and there had been considerable financial reconstruction – but, despite all these changes, profits were still very low. Soon after the government came to power in 1980 and announced a privatisation programme, senior managers began to think about the possibility of a management-led buyout. By early 1981, this idea was being discussed in internal papers. Given the substantial liabilities and pension-fund deficiencies of the company, it was clear that further restructuring would be required. In June 1981, a bank came forward with the conditional offer to finance an employee buyout and the managers gave the company's 25,000 employees a paper explaining the proposition. Between then and October 1981, lengthy negotiations were conducted, described by the Chief Executive in vivid terms: '500 staff meetings, 30 lawyers, 25 civil servants, 6 management briefings, 3 Queen's Counsel, 2 secretaries of state, 1 Act of Parliament and 4 months later, I came to realise that it wasn't quite as simple as I thought' (quoted in S. McLachlan, *The National Freight Buy-out*, Macmillan, London, 1983).

From early in 1981, the government indicated its attraction to such an employee buyout, despite the fact that nothing on this scale had previously been contemplated in the UK. Slowly, the problems with the pension fund and valuation were sorted out and a prospectus was written, which was sufficiently clear to explain not only the complicated financial restructuring involved, but also the employee share trust (which was set up to conduct trading) and the complex loan agreements. Eventually, some 80 per cent of the equity of the company was offered to the employees (with the remaining proportion allotted to the banks who were putting up the loans). Throughout, there was intensive press coverage and a constant stream of seminars between management and employees, with managers taking video presentations to over 700 locations.

The prospectus was published in January 1982, and accompanied by further video presentations. Despite a slow start, the offer was eventually oversubscribed by about £800,000, and attracted altogether some £7 million from the workforce. In the end, the government received almost no net payment since, of the £54 million in debt and equity raised by the consortium, £47 million was used to remedy deficiencies in the pension fund. Almost certainly, if the company had been sold to the general public, let alone to a competing private sector firm, the price would have attracted hostile comments, as it was far under the 'book value' of the company. However, with more than 10,000 shareholders coming from amongst the employees, their families, and pensioners the reaction was almost universally favourable. The extent of the enthusiasm and involvement generated among the workforce and their relations is well represented by a conversation recorded at a subsequent shareholders meeting:

'What would your reaction have been right at the beginning if your husband had come home from work one night and said he wanted to take out a second mortgage on the house to buy shares in his own company?' Answer (Manager's wife): 'Oh, but we did take out a second mortgage. It was my idea' (McLachlan, op. cit.).

The subsequent history of the National Freight Corporation has become a matter of national record. Shares valued at £1.65 in June 1982 were revalued to £2.00 in October 1982, and revalued again to £2.45 in February 1983 and, with a one-for-one bonus issue, were effectively revalued to £3.20 in April 1983. Profits rose by some 50 per cent between 1982–3 and 1983–4, and by 70 per cent between 1984–5 and 1985–6. Even more striking was the change in employee attitudes. When an independent journalist questioned a shop steward about whether the employees who failed to buy shares in the initial offer should be given an opportunity to make up for their error of judgement:

'Not bloody likely' came the explosive reply. 'Not even at £2 a share . . . we took the risk and it was a risk – therefore we should get the reward. Every new employee should be allowed the opportunity to buy shares – that's only fair but not people who had the opportunity first time round and didn't take it' (McLachlan, op. cit.).

Perhaps the most innovative of all the UK management–

93

employee buyouts was the privatisation of Hoverspeed, a company running hovercraft across the Channel, which was jointly owned by British Rail and the Swedish shipping line, Brostrom. The company had several hundred employees and was linked to British Rail's network, but it suffered from continuing losses and operational difficulties. In 1984, there were ideas that Brostrom might take over British Rail's 50 per cent stake. However, Hoverspeed's cash crisis coincided with financial difficulties for Brostrom and the plan was abandoned. In February 1984, when Hoverspeed shares were still given a considerable value in the books of British Rail and Brostrom, it was decided to transfer the company to the private sector and to put it in the hands of a management group. The surprising feature of the operation was that, reflecting its status as a loss-maker, the price for the company paid by the management group for British Rail's 50 per cent share was a nominal £1. The management group was backed by a major commercial bank and almost immediately increased the scale of its operations. Although there were objections to this give-away, criticism of the move appears to have been limited. It remains a unique and relatively short-lived experiment: after reporting a pre-tax profit of £194,000 at the end of 1985, Hoverspeed was taken over by a private sector competitor, Sealink British Ferries, in November 1986, with significant profits for the new shareholders.

Employee buyouts have also been considered in various other countries as a method of privatisation, though they have not yet been used to anything like the same extent as in the UK. In Canada and Turkey, plans have been discussed but sales of this form do not appear to have taken place. In Estonia, profit-orientated worker-run consortia are reported to have taken over TV and radio repairs from the state. In France, employees formed a consortium to take over the TFI TV channel in January 1987 – but gave up the attempt the following month. Somewhat more successfully, the Institut de Développement Industriel, the nationalised development agency, has been sold to a consortium of employees, accompanied by substantial institutional lenders, in a complex structure of holding companies.

An interesting example of the increasing effect of employee buyouts, even in countries where they have not yet been successfully used·as a means of achieving privatisation, comes from Quebec, where, in 1986, the employees of Quebecair, a regional airline owned by the Quebec government, objected to the government's privatisation plans (which involved sale to an existing private sector company) and instead offered C\$9 million, with backing from Air Canada. The employees argued that sale to the private sector competitor would eventually result in the dismantling of the airline and massive redundancies. However, the private competitor undercut the employees' arguments by offering a substantial (16.7 per cent) tranche of employee ownership with a possibility of an increase in employee ownership to twice this level if the company became profitable – indicating vividly the extent to which even commercial purchasers of privatised entities outside the UK are beginning to be aware of the tremendous political advantages attaching to forms of privatisation which involve substantial employee participation.

Public Offers

Employee buyouts are not, however, by any means the only – or indeed the major – way in which employees have become involved in privatisation. Major public offerings of large corporations have brought hundreds of thousands of employees into the process, along with millions of individual shareholders – creating a vast new vested interest in privatisation.

This has, indeed, become the most distinctive form of privatisation, which has attracted far more popular attention than any other, both in the UK and elsewhere. It is also by far the most technically demanding option. The risks involved in such a public offer, both for the government and for the employees and small investors whom the government is trying to attract, make it necessary to choose a candidate with great care. The intrinsic difficulties associated with a major public offer also make it necessary to minimise, as far as possible, the extrinsic complexities and problems. Ease and difficulty in this connection depend principally on two considerations: the financial state of the company and its market position. Promoting a public offer for a company in a poor financial state is both risky and complicated.

Major restructuring may well be needed to make the company saleable – this can involve closures, redundancies and financial changes, since investors may be reluctant to take up shares unless debt is written off and remaining assets are valued realistically. In the meanwhile, the government may encounter opposition from the workforce and management who can feel that their position is threatened and who may become increasingly resentful as re-structuring proceeds. All of these problems are reduced (or eliminated) if the company is in good financial condition: major restructuring will probably not be needed; investors will be queuing up; and the workforce will not feel threatened.

The disadvantages of a public offer for a company with a monopolistic market position may be less obvious but are equally significant. A state monopoly can be defended politically as being 'in the national interest': if it makes large profits, these flow back to the treasury and are returned to the people in the form of public spending, lower public borrowing or reduced taxation. When the monopoly is privatised this case can no longer be argued; any large profits flow into the hands of investors and are presented as exploitation of the customer. Elaborate regulatory mechanisms are, therefore, required to restrain prices and profits. The creation of such regulatory mechanisms in connection with a public offer involves extensive and complex legislation giving ample opportunity for substantial political debate. If, on the other hand, the company being privatised is wholly non-monopolistic – a competitor in a balanced market – these problems disappear: large profits are regarded as a symptom of efficiency rather than a symptom of exploitation; there is no political argument for extensive regulation; and any attacks on privatisation from competitors can be dismissed as special pleading.

The selection of targets for public offer can therefore be represented in a simple matrix:

Less easy	Easy	Non-monopolistic
Difficult	Less easy	Monopolistic
Poor financial condition	Good financial condition	

96

Within the 'easy' group of thriving, non-monopolistic companies various subsidiary features help a public offer on its way. The most important of these is the presence of a chief executive enthusiastic about privatisation. British and French experience indicates that a chief executive who opposes privatisation can prove almost as big an obstacle as a poor financial record or a monopolistic market position. The chief executive is an obvious source of information for journalists, either overtly or covertly; he will be in possession of all relevant facts and will be able to limit their availability to others, will be able to influence other managers and the workforce in numerous ways, will probably have powerful political friends and may well have close connections with the civil service.

Other important (and fairly obvious) catalysts for a successful public offer are: the presence of senior managers who have good relations with officials and are sympathetic to the policy; unions which are on good terms with the government and with management; an intelligent, independent and well-paid workforce, who will regard privatisation as an opportunity rather than as an incomprehensible threat; and a product which is not regarded as a symbol of national pride. The first five major British public offers – BP, British Aerospace, Cable and Wireless, Amersham International and Britoil – all fell into the 'easy' category and had most of these other features. All the public offers in France have shared the same features – though the French government decided to change many of the chief executives in order to ensure their compliance.

Apart from choosing the right target for public offers, the most important catalyst for success is the timetable. The British Treasury has produced an outline timetable of beautiful rationality, moving smoothly from feasibility studies and option papers through ministerial decisions to the selection of advisers, the preparation of the business and of accompanying legislation, the rearrangement of the balance sheet, the choice of market slot, the production of a prospectus, the building of the company's image, and the final sale. This is a highly idealised picture of what actually occurs in privatisation by public offer. In practice, the whole process is bound to be plagued by hesitations and doubts. There are often prolonged arguments about the structure, both commercial and financial, which often come to a head late in the process as the various parties to the transaction begin to realise the implications of early decisions. The market is never static, leading to fears that the wrong timing has been chosen or that further restructuring is necessary, and the condition of the company itself can alter substantially in the course of preparation for the offer. In the early years of the British programme, there were constant arguments and great indecision. Even once the programme had been well developed, some public offers remained highly contentious within government. The British Airways sale was halted and restarted a number of times, as new litigation threatened huge liabilities, and changes in route agreements with other countries were made. The projected public offer of the Royal Ordnance Factories never took place, because it was decided that the financial condition of the company was not sufficiently strong. Similar problems have occurred in other countries. For example, when privatising SOQUEM, the Quebec government at first intended to sell the whole of this large mining conglomerate, then decided that the salt mines could not form part of a public offer, created a new entity known as Cambior which grouped together the company's gold and niobium interests, delayed when no one could decide who had the power to make final decisions, suffered months of anxiety as gold prices wobbled, and finally benefited from an unexpectedly buoyant market and a last-minute rise in the price of gold. The federal government in Canada, meanwhile, has spent years considering the difficulties associated with the public offer of Petro-Canada and Air Canada, while the Turkish government spent almost two years conducting a study of privatisation in general before acquiring either the confidence to select targets or a bureaucratic arrangement for making decisions. In short, the notion of a clear timetable, in which governments proceed rationally through various well-ordered stages is largely fictitious.

Nevertheless, timetabling is vital. The complexities of a public offer are sufficient to deter any government from engaging in the exercise unless there is a timetable which gives the process impetus and sets deadlines for decisions and negotiations. The length of these timetables can, of course, vary widely from case to case. The two ends of the spectrum are well illustrated by the timetables of British Gas in the UK and the National Commercial Bank in Jamaica. In the Jamaican case, the entire exercise took some 12 weeks:

Late September	Ministerial decision to privatise
October	Drafting of all documents
23 October	Review meeting
27 October	Advertising starts
29 October	Pricing decision
7 November	Prospectus issued
3 December	Application list closes
23 December	Dealings commence

At the opposite end of the spectrum, the public offer for British Gas took over eighteen months, even after the basic decisions about the structure of the industry had been made:

May 1985	Ministerial decision to privatise, advisers appointed
September 1985	Drafting of documents commences
July 1986	Gas Bill receives Royal Assent
September 1986	Offer for Sale marketing commences
31 October 1986	Pathfinder prospectus published
21 November 1986	Impact day
3 December 1986	Application list closes
8 December 1986	Dealings commence

Part of the reason for this great difference in time-scale between one public offer and another is the relative complexity of the two exercises. In the case of a major utility such as British Gas or British Telecom, a large amount of legislative activity is required. In the case of British Telecom, for example, an entirely new company had to be created under the Telecommunications Act

1984. The Act gave the Secretary of State the power to transfer all the relevant assets to a 'successor company' and subsequently to issue shares in this company. A similar Act was required to set up the British Columbia Resources Investment Corporation in 1979, to transfer government shareholdings in the component companies to the new corporation, and to establish the terms on which the new company would operate. More recently, in New Zealand, legislation has been required to establish new corporations in the 'corporatisation' process as a prelude to the public offering of 'equity bonds', and complex legislation was also required to establish Nippon Telephone and Telegraph before that public offer could take place in Japan. As a result, all of these privatisations have taken far longer to achieve than the French and Jamaican cases – where no complex legislation was required for each individual entity.

Another vital element in a public offer is the structure of the company itself. On the whole, those British privatisations that have involved the disposal of an entire nationalised industry have not involved any substantial change in the role of the board or in other structural relationships within the company before privatisation. The major exception to this rule has occurred when the statutory position of the company has made it unattractive to private investors. In such cases, a holding company or some other such device has been used to distance the asset holder from the operating company – as in the case of Associated British Ports. When public offers have involved the disposal of part of a nationalised concern, however, structural change has been more usual. In the case of Jaguar, for example, the relationship with its parent company, British Leyland, had to be radically altered before a public offer.

Typically, those responsible for public offers in the UK have also attempted to minimise changes in senior personnel. Executive directors of nationalised industries being offered for sale, who are generally appointees of the relevant Secretary of State, have been kept in place throughout the process. Only those Civil Servants who have acted as non-executive directors before privatisation have generally left the board at the moment of privatisation. In France, the pattern has been rather different. As part of preparation for its rapid programme of public offers, the

French government decided in July 1986 to replace the chief executives of three industrial companies, seven banks and two insurance companies. Remarkably, this painful process was achieved with relatively little adverse publicity – perhaps partly because it relied to some extent on a game of musical chairs, in which some of those relinquishing a post in one public sector company took up a position in another.

The creation of new corporations and the realignment of personnel are, however, minor matters compared to the establishment of regulation, which has been required to prepare for public offers of utilities and other monopolies. Three major forms of utility regulation are used around the world, straightforward cost-plus restrictions (which allow the utility to charge customers a set margin over costs), comparisons with international market prices (which constrain the prices paid by domestic consumers by reference to other comparable imported products) and, most common of all, rate-of-return restrictions (which prevent utilities from making 'superprofits' by allowing only a given return on net assets). In practice, straightforward cost-plus measures have been regarded as too crude in sophisticated economies, and market-based measures have been considered too unstable. Rate-of-return regulation has, therefore, been used extensively in countries as different from one another as New Zealand, Hong Kong and the USA. However, experience of rate-of-return regulation, particularly in the USA, where it has become a highly developed art, suggested to the British government that it might not be an appropriate way of constraining utilities if they were to be privatised by public offer. Rate-of-return regulation suffers from a long history of disadvantages: it leaves open wide areas of discretion about matters such as the cost of capital and the form of current cost to be taken into account; it frequently penalises the utility more heavily than intended due to the difficulty of predicting future performance; it involves a large amount of time and money spent regularly on public hearings; it tends either to induce over-investment by giving undue bonuses for increases in the asset base, or else to impose unpredictable and extremely tough disincentives for investment; it provides few incentives for efficiency; it maintains no direct control over prices; it encourages 'short-termism'; and it tends to lead to ever-greater interference by the regulatory authorities in activities which are unregulated. As a result of these notorious deficiencies, the British government was concerned that investors would be reluctant to take up public offers for companies subject to rate-of-return regulation. A prolonged investigation was consequently set in train, with contributions from the Prime Minister's Economic Adviser, the Department of Trade and Industry, and an independent consultant, the now famous Professor Littlechild. After considering the possibility of an output-related profits levy, which would have syphoned off superprofits whilst still giving companies an incentive to innovate and grow, Professor Littlechild (and subsequently the government itself) decided to adopt instead an innovative form of price regulation. This is contained in the so-called 'RPI$-x$' formula, which keeps annual price increases for a defined basket of utility services in line with the increase in the retail price index less a set percentage, providing a stimulus for real-terms cost cutting. Though in concept simple, this RPI$-x$ formula is by no means so simple in practice, as is indicated by the detailed excerpt from the Authorisation for British Gas contained in Appendix 4. Months of time and effort have been required to sort out the details of the formula in connection with each major utility privatisation in the UK, and to ensure that the presentation of the formula in the prospectus can be understood by investors. However, the formula – with numerous additions and changes – has been applied not only to British Telecom but also to British Gas and the British Airports Authority, and has amply proved itself a successful means of allaying investors' fears about the unpredictability of regulation on privatised utilities. Whether similar forms of regulation will be chosen in other countries when they, too, come to privatise utilities (as now seems almost certain to occur) remains to be seen.

The legislative framework is, however, only part of the preparation required before a major privatisation by offer for sale can take place. Given the enormous risks being run by the government in so public an activity, it is vital to ensure that both the government and potential investors have a clear picture of the nature of the company being privatised and of all the elements of its commercial and financial position which could affect its long-term value. The sheer information requirements of this exercise are daunting, as can be seen from the outline of a long-form accountant's report of the kind used in the major UK offers for sale (Appendix 5).

Information is just the first stage of the process. Long and difficult arguments about the structuring of the balance sheet follow. Nationalised companies are often highly geared: the government is willing to tolerate this because, acting both as equity-holder and as lender, it is indifferent between interest and dividend. The private investor in a public offer for sale is obviously in a different position. The debt–equity ratio will be a prime concern for him, and major restructuring is therefore often needed. This is particularly important if the business is in a very competitive market sector with cyclical demand. The financial gearing level has to be reduced so that the business is not burdened both with a high operating ratio and a high debt–equity ratio. In principle, these are technical matters which should cause little trouble, since the proceeds received by the government from the sale ought to increase to the extent that the government has written off debt or has injected equity. However, due to national accounting constraints and public appearances, this view is often not taken by ministers and officials. 'Writing off debt' and 'injecting equity' sound as if they involve a net public sector cost, and may well appear in this guise to the national bookkeepers. In Canada, for example, the book value of a public sector company in national accounts reflects the total investment made by the government in that company over the years – leading to night-marish effects on official public spending figures if certain forms of restructuring are carried out.

In addition to the government's problems, the company about to be privatised has its own point of view. It almost always argues in favour of practically no debt, since this will give it the capacity to engage in aggressive acquisitions immediately following priva-tisation. Debates about gearing levels in the preparation for a public offer for sale have consequently taken days and nights in closed rooms and have often reached the public arena. Contin-gent and concealed liabilities have also caused endless difficul-ties. In particular, index-linked pensions offered by nationalised industries to their employees have frequently turned out to be under-funded, requiring adjustments before the offer for sale can proceed. Exchange risks related to debt are also a major bone of contention in some cases. When privatising the Caribbean Cement Company, for example, the Jamaican government was forced to accommodate the problem by redenominating US dollar debt into Jamaican debt before the offer for sale.

While the preparation of the company is proceeding, important decisions about the structure of the offer itself need to be made. In particular, the government and its advisers have to decide how much to sell (the percentage of the company to be sold in one tranche, the percentage of the purchase price to be paid in one instalment, and the volume that can be absorbed by the market); how to sell it (whether by fixed price offer, or by tender, or by a mixture of the two); to whom it should be sold (the proportions allocated to domestic institutions, small individuals, employees and the overseas market); what incentive should be given (the discounts available for employees, bonuses available for individuals retaining their shares over a given period, and any other *douceurs* such as discounts on bills for those who buy shares in a utility); how to handle any overseas tranche (making predictions of overseas demand, assessing the relationship of the overseas offer to the domestic offer and allocating between different countries); and finally what price to charge (involving the prediction of sustainable earnings, the adoption of a given measure such as the price–earnings ratio and the final, critical, judgement of market perception).

None of these matters can be resolved by science. All involve judgement, case by case, and the permutations have been endless. The aggregate amounts sold in such offers around the world have varied between £25 million and over £5,000 million. The proportion of the company offered has ranged from under 5 to 100 per cent. Purchase prices per share have varied from 20p to £40. In some cases, the purchase price has been paid all at once; in other cases it has been paid in two or three instalments. Price–earnings ratios have varied widely – as one would expect given the different natures of the different companies being privatised. The proportion allotted to employees in a given offer has varied between 2 and 100 per cent. The amounts allocated to overseas markets have varied between 0 and 20 per cent. Employee share schemes have been constructed in various different ways (see p.47 and Appendix 2) and the treatment of institutions *vis-à-vis* individuals has altered from case to case, not least because every known method from fixed price offers to tenders and combinations of the two have been used. Pricing has been as erratic as was inevitable given the complexity of the predictions involved, with some offers less than 30 per cent subscribed and others 30–40 times oversubscribed, leading to opening prices representing between a 20 per cent drop and a 90 per cent premium.

The design of the offer with all its bewildering complexity is, however, by no means the end of such a privatisation. Indeed, it is not even the beginning. Like every other commodity, shares in nationalised industries being offered to the public need not only to be correctly designed, but also to be marketed. The choice of target, the establishment of a timetable, the preparation, the legislative framework of the company and the design of the offer itself are merely the prelude: the play itself consists of the selling of the shares.

The prospectus, over which an immense amount of time and energy is lavished, is a minor element in this marketing campaign. It exists largely to ensure that the investor is able to warn himself (if he so chooses) about the risks he is taking. Nevertheless, with a sale to the public by the government, there can be no chance of a failure to disclose any conceivably relevant fact. The British Gas prospectus, for example, with its 80 closely printed pages, is a minor masterpiece of business analysis. It describes in detail the activity of the company, the historical background, the market for gas, the competitive position in which the company finds itself, the nature of gas supplies and the supply network, the company's research and development programme, its organisation and management, its employees and their pensions and, of course, its financial condition down to the last iota; there are special sections on the relationship between the company and the government, the regulatory environment, the reports of experts including the accountants and petroleum consultants, and painstaking descriptions of all aspects of the offer.

It is the advertising campaigns for public offers rather than the prospectuses that have caught the public's attention. Not only in the UK but also in France, Jamaica, Japan and the USA, a new level of professionalism and imagination has been achieved in these advertising programmes. Again, British Gas provides a classic example. After a sustained programme of advertisements about the company itself there was a further series stressing the ability of every man and woman to participate in the offer and then, as a magnificent *coup de grâce*, the mythical figure of Sid was introduced to increase public interest. In the last few days, British Gas itself virtually disappeared from the scene – Sid came to dominate. Indeed, one of the last sequence of advertisements contained simply the word 'Sid'!

Accompanying this extravaganza of the advertiser's art is the patient construction of distribution systems to accommodate these massive public offers, as well as registration systems capable of dealing not only with the level of trading to be anticipated from a share held by millions of individuals but also with the enforcement of the special regulations built into every offer for political reasons. Altogether, these exercises have been conducted with the precision of military manoeuvres by armies of professionals.

The results have been commensurate with the effort. True, major public offers had been used as methods of privatisation in only eight countries by late 1987 (the UK, France, West Germany, Japan, USA, Canada, New Zealand and Jamaica). But they had accounted for the great majority of the assets privatised in the entire world – some £50 billion's worth in all. They had attracted over 25 million investors. And they had given over a million employees a stake in their companies. No other method could have been remotely so complex; nor could any other method have been remotely so successful as a means of creating a vested interest in favour of privatisation. By creating that favourable lobby of small investors and employees, public offers have brought privatisation into its own, endowing it with the power to make an indelible imprint on the economic history of the twentieth century.

5

THE FUTURE?

The story of privatisation is by no means yet complete. The fast and far-reaching changes which have taken place in the last eight years seem destined to continue and perhaps even accelerate over the next two or three years, as countries which have been planning and taking the first tentative steps launch full-scale programmes involving major public offers. In the UK, already well ahead of the game, there is every sign that the programme will intensify, sweeping out of the public sector the remaining utilities, perhaps also significant parts of the steel, rail and coal industries, and no doubt dozens of other smaller assets. There are indications that tougher regulation and more emphasis on competition will be built into the programme. And it seems possible – though by no means certain – that the number of shareholders will again leap upwards, perhaps reaching the point where more than half of the adult population have a direct stake in the capital market.

In the rest of Europe, France seems destined to be joined by Austria, Spain, Portugal and Turkey, with their significant state sectors and their relatively undeveloped capital markets. It seems altogether likely that the structure of their economies will be altered as much or more than those of the UK and France by the end of the process. Further to the east, Singapore, Malaysia and the Philippines look set to become major players, with Sri Lanka and possibly India to follow. Japan's programme may well dwarf that of the rest of the world in money terms, and further south both Australia and New Zealand look as if they are only at the beginings of large-scale programmes.

The great question marks hang over Africa and the Americas. With dozens of studies now being conducted, the Africans could be on the verge of serious privatisation programmes. In the Americas, other Caribbean countries may well begin to emulate Jamaica's remarkable achievements; and Mexico and Brazil may well join Chile in the league of the mass privatisers, changing gear from trade sales to public offers. Almost certainly they will be preceded by Canada, where the provinces (if not the federal government) are setting about privatisation with gusto.

As the fashion spreads, and as each country applies the lessons from others in its own way, new techniques are bound to be developed and to come into prominence. New forms of regulation for monopolies will almost certainly emerge. New uses for debt-for-equity schemes will doubtless be found, linking them more firmly with privatisation. New forms of capital market will be constructed, where previously none existed or where the level of development is low. There will be new attacks, as yet unanticipated, from new classes of opponent, and new methods of defence. These are easy things to predict because the trend is so marked, the volume so great, and the momentum so powerful. It is far more difficult to guess what will happen at the end of the decade, as the 1980s turn into the 1990s. The patterns of growth and inflation to which we have become accustomed in the 1980s may not continue. As bull markets give way to pessimism, new fashions, intellectual and political, may begin to affect economists and politicians around the world.

And if there is a change in mood, if the balance stops shifting towards the private sector, will it then shift back again? How reversible will the process prove to be? In theory, the creation of increasing numbers of new shareholders and employees with stakes in their company should provide a natural brake on any attempts at renationalisation. But that theory may prove to be false. Perhaps, with bear markets and worsening economic conditions, investors will become disillusioned and what was once popular capitalism will become unpopular loss-making. Perhaps, on the contrary, the momentum will be so great by the end of the 1980s that it carries privatisation forward into the 1990s with increasing speed. Perhaps governments of every hue will come to accept dominance by the private sector as a natural phenomenon, in much the same way that, over the past 40 years, they came to accept and take for granted the power of the public sector. These are irresolvable questions. The only certainty is that the future of privatisation will be at least as interesting as its past.

APPENDIX 1

Advertising

The Thatcher government's privatisation programme has been designed to appeal especially to the small investor – the 'man in the street' who may never have owned shares in the past. As a result, each flotation has been accompanied by a high-profile advertising campaign with such memorable features as TSB's bowler hat ('you, too, can be a banker'), British Telecom's knotted phones ('don't forget the last day for share applications') and of course, the ubiquitous 'Sid' (originally blissfully unaware of the British Gas flotation and now more or less a household name).

The flotation of Rolls-Royce, however, shows quite a different kind of campaign. As a company with a name chiefly associated with one of the most exclusive cars in the world, the public had to be made aware that this particular Rolls-Royce had nothing to do with the manufacture of cars. The result was a series of advertisements depicting aero-engines, with the emphasis on the reliability and general technological excellence of the main product of the company.

The advertisements reproduced in the following pages are a small representative sample, indicating the different sorts of appeal that have been made so successfully to the public.

THE MINIMUM INVESTMENT FOR BRITISH GAS SHARES WILL BE NO MORE THAN £150. BUT YOU CAN APPLY FOR A LOT MORE.

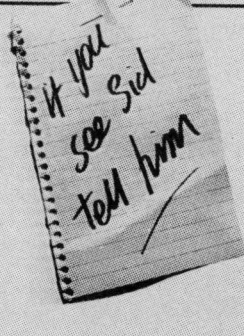

We want as many people as possible to be able afford British Gas shares, so we're making the minimum investment level as low as possible.

It won't be more than £150, and you won't have find that all at once, because payment will be by talments. If you want to apply for a lot more than 50 worth of shares, you can, of course.

The important thing is to make sure you're ready when it's time to apply in late November.

If you're interested in a share of the shares, simply fill in the coupon on this page or phone 0272 272 272.

In return, you will be sent an information pack and updated information when it becomes available.

This won't commit you in any way, but it will ensure that you are sent a prospectus and an application form when they're published. Which will save you a lot of bother later on.

Everyone can apply for a share of the shares.

ISSUED BY N M ROTHSCHILD & SONS LIMITED ON BEHALF OF H M GOVERNMENT

YOU HAVE ONLY 4 DAYS TO GET YOUR APPLICATION IN FOR BRITISH GAS SHARES.

Postal applications must be received by 10am next <u>Wednesday, December 3rd.</u> Use first class post and allow at least 2 days for delivery.

Alternatively, hand in your application at any UK branch of NatWest, Bank of Scotland or Ulster Bank before close of business next <u>Tuesday, December 2nd.</u>

Hurry if you want to apply for a share of the shares.

British Gas
SHARE
INFORMATION
OFFICE

UP AGAINST TIME by Jeanne Willis and Trevor Melvin

113

JOIN OUR FAN CLUB.

You're looking at a Rolls-Royce wide-chord fan.

It has fewer, wider blades than the engines made by our competitors. And it makes our engine more powerful, more economical and quieter.

The design, development, testing and manufacture of this entirely new type of fan is a Rolls-Royce achievement.

It is used on our latest engines for the Boeing 747 and 757.

Currently over 270 of the world's airlines use Rolls-Royce engines. So do more than 110 defence forces. We also make gas turbines for ships and industry.

We employ 42,000 people directly, and through our 500 suppliers we provide work for many thousands more.

In 1985 our pre-tax profits hit a record £81 million from sales of £1.6 billion. Our results for 1986 will be out shortly.

Quite soon you will be able to apply for shares in Rolls-Royce. If you would like more information, call 01-200 3000 or send the coupon.

You will then receive a Rolls-Royce brochure and a prospectus when it is issued.

Please send me further information on Rolls-Royce, and a Prospectus when available.

Name
Address
Town
County .... Postcode

When complete, send to: The Rolls-Royce Share Information Office, PO Box 365, Liverpool L69 3BR. Or telephone 01-200 3000.

A SHARE IN BRITISH EXCELLENCE.

114

AFTER 18 YEARS WE STILL HAVE THE JUMP ON OUR COMPETITORS.

Over the years a number of manufacturers around the world have had a go at out-jumping us.

All their efforts seem to have fallen by the wayside.

The Harrier, which is powered by the Rolls-Royce Pegasus engine, is the only vertical take-off and landing fixed wing aircraft in service. The RAF, the Royal Navy, the Spanish and Indian navies all fly Harriers.

The US Marine Corps, which already operates 68 AV8B Harriers, wants more than 300.

Currently over 110 of the world's defence forces use Rolls-Royce engines. So do more than 270 airlines.

Last year pre-tax profits hit a record £120 million from sales of £1·8 billion.

Quite soon you will be able to apply for shares in Rolls-Royce.

If you would like more information, call 01-200 3000 or send the coupon.

You will then receive a Rolls-Royce brochure and a prospectus when it is issued.

115

APPENDIX 2

Employee Share Schemes

Privatised companies in the UK operate a number of different forms of employee share schemes. An illustration of the sorts of provision found in each of the three types is given below.

It should be noted that: no one scheme conforms precisely to these illustrations; many of the privatised companies operate more than one type of scheme; and all the schemes are subject to limits governing the number of shares that can be issued under them – normally preventing even those schemes that are open to all employees from involving more than 5–10 percent of the company's shares.

Discretionary Share schemes governed by Trustees

Full-time employees (i.e. those working a minimum number of (usually 30) hours per week), who have completed a given period of service (e.g. 12 months) up to a qualifying date set by directors, are normally eligible to take part in the scheme. The scheme is typically constituted by a trust deed which provides for an employee share ownership scheme to be operated in either or both of the following ways:

1. The company may provide the trustees each year with funds to enable them to subscribe and/or purchase ordinary shares which will then be appropriated to eligible employees who have indicated that they wish to participate in the scheme. The amount of funds thus made available and the amount available for each individual employee will be determined by the directors.

2. Eligible employees may be invited to contribute funds which will be used by the trustees to acquire ordinary shares on their behalf.

116

The scheme comes into operation at the time of share issue a.. the option to make use of it again is available annually. The directors decide whether the share ownership scheme is to be operated in any year and, if so, the proportion or amount of the company's profits of the relevant financial year to be allocated to that scheme, which may not exceed a stated percentage of the profits of the company.

The maximum value of shares which may be appropriated to any participant under the share ownership scheme in any year is explicitly limited and the shares issued under the share ownership scheme must be held by the trustees for a minimum period of two years after appropriation, during which they may not be dealt with in any way except in certain circumstances such as death, reaching statutory pensionable age or ceasing to be an employee through injury, disability or redundancy. For the following three years the trustees must retain the shares unless a participant instructs them otherwise and thereafter the shares may be transferred to the participant.

Savings Related Share Option Schemes

Employees may enter into a Save-As-You-Earn contract, agreeing to make regular contributions of their choice (subject to a minimum and a maximum). Each employee joining the scheme is granted an option to subscribe to ordinary shares in the company. The price to be paid is determined by the directors, but cannot be less than a stated percentage (e.g. 90 per cent) of the average market value of such shares on the few latest practicable business days before the date of the offer of participation.

Executive Share Option Scheme

Options may be granted to full-time employees and executive directors who are not within two years of their contractual retirement date. Participation is normally limited to those individuals who can be expected to make a distinctive contribution to profit performance (e.g. the 50 senior executives).

Options may generally only be granted in a set period following the announcement of the interim or final results. The minimum

117

subscription price is fixed by the directors, but must not be less than the average market price of a share over a period of three business days ending on the third business day before the date of grant. No individual may normally be granted options over shares with an aggregate subscription price exceeding a set multiple of his annual relevant emoluments.

APPENDIX 3

*Limiting the Size of Shareholdings without
the Use of a Special Share*

**Provisions made in Clause 4 of the Memorandum of the
National Commercial Bank Group Limited, Jamaica**

Notwithstanding anything contained herein or in the Articles of
Association of the Company and in furtherance of the objects of
the Company the following provisions shall have effect:

A. (i) The Company shall not sell, transfer, assign, dispose of
or create any charge on any of the shares of any of its
subsidiaries carrying on banking business as defined in
the Bank Act, except by the authority of a resolution
unanimously passed at an extraordinary general meeting
at which there are present, in person or by proxy,
members together holding 90% of the issued shares
carrying voting rights in the Relevant Share Capital as
defined in sub-clause F of this Clause.

(ii) Where either the Company or any subsidiary carries on
banking business as defined above, the Company shall
ensure that neither the Company nor any such subsidiary shall sell, transfer, assign or dispose of such a
substantial part of its assets as may materially adversely
affect the banking business carried on by the Company
or that subsidiary, and shall further ensure that neither
the Company nor any such subsidiary creates, other than
in the ordinary course of business, any legal or equitable
charge on its assets that could result in the acquisition by
another of such substantial part of its assets as may
materially adversely affect its banking business, EX-
CEPT, in either case, by the authority of a resolution

unanimously passed at an extraordinary general meeting of the Company, at which there are present, in person or in proxy, members together holding 90% of the voting rights in the relevant share capital as defined in sub-clause F of this Clause.

B. (i) Without prejudice to any special rights previously conferred on the holders of any existing shares or class of shares, the Company may by ordinary resolution, as the Company may from time to time determine, issue any shares with rights and restrictions identical to those attaching to the Ordinary Shares of the Company.

    (ii) Without prejudice to any special rights previously conferred on the holders of any existing shares or class of shares, the Company may by ordinary resolution issue shares other than ordinary shares with such preferred, deferred or other special rights, or such restrictions in regard to dividend or return of capital as the Company may from time to time determine.

    (iii) Shares issued under paragraph (ii) above shall not entitle the holders (a) to vote upon any resolution (other than a resolution for winding up the Company or reducing its share capital) unless at the date of the notice convening the meeting at which such resolution is to be proposed, the dividend on such shares is six months or more in arrears, or (b) to receive notice of or to attend at any General Meeting unless the business of the meeting includes the consideration of a resolution upon which such holders are entitled to vote. Nor shall such shares or any loan stock or debentures of the Company be converted into Ordinary Shares, except where the conversion is such that the market value of each unit of such shares, loan stock or debentures is equal to the market value of the Ordinary Shares into which that unit is converted.

    (iv) Notwithstanding sub-paragraphs (ii) and (iii) of this paragraph, the Company may not issue any shares with voting rights attached thereto, not being shares with rights identical with those attaching to the Ordinary Shares unless the voting rights attached to these shares

120

when aggregated with all other such shares constitute not more than five percent of the maximum number of votes capable of being cast on a poll at any General Meeting (in whatever circumstances and for whatever purpose the same may have been convened).

C. Subject to the provisions of Section 57 of the Act or any modification thereof, and subject to sub-clause B of this Clause, preference shares may, with the sanction of an ordinary resolution, be issued on the terms that they are, or are liable at the option of the Company, to be redeemed on such terms and in such a manner as the Company before the issue of the shares may by special resolution determine.

D. (i) If at any time the share capital is divided into different classes of shares, the rights attached to any class (unless otherwise provided by the terms of issue of the shares of that class) may, whether or not the Company is being wound up, be varied with the consent in writing of the holders of three-fourths of the issued shares of that class, or with the sanction of an extraordinary resolution passed at a separate general meeting of the holders of the shares of the class PROVIDED that no such variation shall in any way contravene or be capable of resulting at any time in a contravention of any of the provisions of sub-clause B of this Clause.

(ii) To every such separate general meeting the provisions of this Clause relating to general meetings shall apply *mutatis mutandis*.

E. The rights conferred upon the holders of the shares of any class issued with preferred or other rights shall not be deemed to be varied by the creation or issue of further shares ranking *pari passu* therewith.

F. (i) For the purposes of this sub-clause and sub-clause G:
   (1) 'Relevant Share Capital' means issued share capital carrying any right to vote at a general meeting of the Company provided that for the purposes of voting at general meetings of the Company this definition shall not include shares in which the right to vote has been temporarily suspended.

121

(2) A person shall be taken to have an interest in shares, if:

   (a) he is a legal or beneficial owner of these shares; or

   (b) he enters into a contract for the purchase by him of these shares (whether for cash or other consideration); or

   (c) not being the registered holder, he is entitled to exercise any right conferred by the holding of these shares or is entitled to control the exercise of any such right; or

   (d) he has the right to call for the delivery of these shares to himself or to his order; or

   (e) he has a contractual right to acquire an interest in the shares or is under an obligation to take an interest in these shares or has a contingent interest in these shares; or

   (f) his spouse or any infant child or infant step child of his has an interest in these shares; or

   (g) a body corporate has an interest in these shares and the body corporate or its Board, or other governing body are accustomed to act in accordance with his directions or instructions; or

   (h) he is entitled to exercise or control the exercise of one-third or more of the voting power at general meetings of that body corporate; or

   (i) he is entitled to control a body corporate that is entitled, either directly or through control of other bodies corporate, to exercise or control the voting power at general meetings of a body corporate which is the owner of the shares; or

   (j) he is involved in an agreement (legally binding or which involves mutuality in the undertakings expectations or understanding of the parties to it) for the acquisition of the shares with another party, in which case the interest of each of the parties shall be taken to be an interest in all of the shares whether or not the shares were acquired pursuant to the agreement.

(ii) Where a person either to his knowledge acquires or ought reasonably to be aware that he has acquired an interest in 5% or more of the Relevant Share Capital he shall within 5 days next after acquiring the interest or within 5 days next after he ought reasonably to become aware that he has acquired the interest notify the Company in writing of the number of shares he has become interested in.

(iii) Where a person to whom paragraph (ii) of this sub-clause applies, to his knowledge increases the number of shares in which he has an interest or ought reasonably to be aware that he has increased the number of shares in which he has an interest, he shall within 5 days next thereafter notify the Company of the alteration in the number of shares in which he has an interest.

(iv) Where a person who has to his knowledge acquired or ought reasonably to have been aware that he has acquired an interest in 5% or more of the Relevant Share Capital and has failed to notify the Company in writing within 5 days as specified in paragraph (ii) of this sub-clause the registered holder of the shares in which such person has an interest shall not for one year next after the service on such registered holder of notice of this fact by the Registrar be entitled to attend or vote at (whether in person or by proxy) any General Meeting of the Company or meeting of the holders of Relevant Share Capital or of any class thereof. The same stipulation shall apply in the case of a person who has failed to notify the Company pursuant to paragraph (iii) of this sub-clause.

(v) Paragraphs (ii), (iii) and (iv) of this sub-clause shall not apply to the acquisition of shares before 8th December 1986, but shall otherwise apply.

G. (i) For the purpose of this sub-clause:

(1) 'Relevant Person' means any person who has, or who appears to the Registrar after consultation with the Company's Attorneys-at-law to have, an interest in shares (in any of the senses referred to in

sub-clause F of this clause) which carry more than 7.5% of the total votes attaching to Relevant Share Capital of all classes taken as a whole;

(2) 'Permitted Person' means:

    (a) a trustee (acting in that capacity) of an employee share scheme of the Company or any of its subsidiaries;

    (b) a trustee (acting in that capacity) who has disclosed the beneficial owners (other than the trustee) or the trust to the Company and who has given, or is irrevocably bound under the terms of the trust to give a voting proxy to such beneficial owners to the intent that the voting rights shall not be exercised by the trustee;

    (c) National Investment Bank of Jamaica Limited (provided that a change of name shall not affect this definition) EXCEPT that this sub-paragraph shall not apply in the case of any shares acquired by the National Investment Bank of Jamaica Limited after the 8th December 1986.

(3) 'Relevant Share Capital' has the meaning assigned to it in sub-clause F of this Clause, excluding however the proviso thereto.

(4) 'Relevant Shares' means all shares in the Relevant Share Capital in which a Relevant Person has or appears to the Registrar, on the advice of the Company's Attorneys-at-law, to have an interest.

(5) 'Registrar' means any person or company appointed by the Company from time to time to act as registrar or registrar and transfer agent.

(6) 'Required Disposal' means a disposal or disposals of such a number of Relevant Shares as will cause a Relevant Person to cease to be a Relevant Person, not being a disposal to another Relevant Person (other than a Permitted Person) or a disposal which constitutes any other person (other than a Permitted Person) a Relevant Person.

(ii) The purpose of this sub-clause is to prevent any person other than a Permitted Person from remaining a Relevant Person. Accordingly, at the earliest opportunity after the amendment of this Memorandum of Association effected on the 4th November 1986 the Board must appoint a Registrar and direct the Registrar to determine on a continuous basis whether any person other than a Permitted Person is or has become a Relevant Person, and to obtain the opinion of the Company's Attorneys-at-law whether such a person is a Relevant Person and to report the matter to the Board. The Board must stipulate that if any person other than a Permitted Person to the knowledge of the Registrar becomes a Relevant Person, the Registrar after consulting with the Company's Attorneys-at-law, shall serve a written notice on all persons (other than Permitted Persons) who appear to the Registrar to have interests in the relevant shares and, if different, on the registered holders of the Relevant Shares. Such notice shall set out the restrictions referred to in paragraph (v) of this sub-clause and call for a Required Disposal to be made within 21 days of the service of the notice on the registered holder.

The Board must also stipulate that the Registrar shall immediately notify the Board in writing when such notice has been served. The Board may also allow but must not direct the Registrar to withdraw such notice (whether before or after the expiration of the period referred to) if the Registrar after consultation with the Company's Attorneys-at-law is of the opinion that there is no Relevant Person in relation to the shares concerned. Upon the giving of such notice, and save for the purpose of a Required Disposal under this paragraph (ii) or the following paragraph (iii), no transfer of any of the Relevant Shares may be registered until either such notice is withdrawn or a Required Disposal has been made to the satisfaction of the Registrar after consultation with the Company's Attorneys-at-law.

(iii) The Board shall also direct that if a notice served under paragraph (ii) of this sub-clause has not been complied with in all respects to the satisfaction of the Registrar after consultation with the Company's Attorneys-at-law and has not been withdrawn, the Registrar shall, so far as he is able, make a Required Disposal and shall give written notice of such disposal to those persons on whom such notice was served.

The Board shall also stipulate that the manner, timing and terms of any such Required Disposal made or sought to be made by the Registrar (including but not limited to the price or prices at which the same is made and the extent to which assurance is obtained that no transferee (with the exception of a Permitted Person) is or would become a Relevant Person) shall be such as the Registrar determines based upon advice from bankers, brokers or other appropriate persons consulted by him for the purpose, to be reasonably practicable having regard to all the circumstances including but not limited to the number of shares to be disposed of and the requirement that the disposal be made without delay; and that the Registrar shall not be liable to any person for any of the consequences of reliance on such advice. The Board shall further direct that if, on a Required Disposal being required to be made by the Registrar, Relevant Shares are held by more than one registered holder (treating joint holders of any Relevant Shares as a single holder) the Registrar shall cause as near as is practicable the same proportion of each registered holding, as is known to the Registrar, of such Relevant Shares to be sold.

(iv) For the purpose of effecting any Required Disposal, the Board may authorise in writing any officer or employee of the Company to execute as directed by the Registrar any necessary transfer and may enter the name of the transferee in respect of the transferred shares in the Register notwithstanding the absence of any share certificate being lodged in connection therewith and may issue a new certificate to the transferee. The net proceeds of such disposal shall be received by the Company whose receipt shall be a good discharge for the purchase money, and shall be paid (without any interest being payable thereon and after deduction of any expenses incurred by the Registrar in the sale) to the former registered holder (or, in the case of joint holders, the first named joint holder thereof in the Register) upon surrender by him or on his behalf of any certificate in respect of the Relevant Shares sold and formerly held by him, which shall then be cancelled. For the purpose of this clause the person executing any transfer shall be deemed to be acting as the attorney for the transferor.

(v) A registered holder of Relevant Shares on whom a notice has been served under this sub-clause G of this Clause shall not in respect of such share be entitled until such time as such notice has been withdrawn or the notice has been complied with to the satisfaction of the Board to attend or vote at (whether in person or by proxy) any General Meeting of the Company or meeting of the holders of Relevant Share Capital or of any class thereof.

(vi) Without prejudice to the provisions of the Act and subject to the provisions of paragraph (i) of this sub-clause the Board shall permit the Registrar to assume without enquiry that a person is not a Relevant Person unless the information contained in the register of members kept by the Company appears to the Registrar to indicate to the contrary or the Registrar has reason to believe otherwise.

(vii) The Board shall not oblige the Registrar to serve any notice required under this sub-clause to be served upon any person if the Registrar does not know either his identity or his address.

The absence of service of such a notice in such circumstances as aforesaid and any accidental error in or failure to give any notice to any person upon whom notice is required to be served under this sub-clause shall not prevent the implementation of or invalidate any procedure under this sub-clause.

(viii) If any director has reason to believe that a person (not being a Permitted Person) is a Relevant Person he shall inform the Registrar of that fact.

(ix) The provision of the Articles of Association as to service of notices given to Members shall apply to notices required by this sub-clause to be given to any person.

(x) Any resolution or determination of, or decision or exercise of any discretion or power by, the Board or the Registrar (including without prejudice to the generality of the foregoing as to what constitutes reasonable enquiry or as to the manner, timing and terms of any Required Disposal made under paragraph (iii) of this sub-clause) shall be final and conclusive and any disposal or transfer made, or other thing done, on behalf of, or on the authority of, the Board or any director pursuant to the foregoing provisions of this sub-clause shall be conclusive and binding on all persons concerned and shall not be open to challenge, whether as to its validity or otherwise on any ground whatsoever.

H. Any member may transfer all or any of this shares in accordance with the Articles of Association provided that any form of transfer used in connection with transfers of over 50,000 shares shall have a declaration on the reverse side by the transferee stating the ultimate beneficial owner of the shares: PROVIDED that a transfer of shares to NIBJ or to the Government as defined in sub-clause J of this Clause shall not be approved by the Board or registered if such transfer will result in either NIBJ or the Government as so defined holding shares in excess of 7.5% of the authorised share capital of the Company. For the avoidance of doubt, the proviso to this sub-clause applies notwithstanding the restriction on voting by NIBJ and the Government described in sub-clause J.

I. Such of the provisions of this Memorandum of Association as are applicable to paid-up shares shall apply to stock and the words 'share' and 'shareholder' therein shall include 'stock' and 'stockholder'.

J. In this clause:

(a) 'NIBJ' shall mean the National Investment Bank of Jamaica Limited and or any successor or assigns of the NIBJ, subsidiaries, parent company or nominees;

(b) 'Government' shall mean the Government of Jamaica and include government agencies, statutory corporations, government controlled companies or anyone acting on behalf of the Government.

As at the 4th November, 1986 (the date of the amendment of this Memorandum of Association) NIBJ was the legal or beneficial owner of all the issued share capital of the Company.

If after that date NIBJ sells some, but not all, of the said shares pursuant to a public Offer for Sale then those shares which remain in its ownership or come into the ownership of Government by direct acquisition from NIBJ, shall not, whilst owned by NIBJ or Government, carry the right to vote at any General Meeting of the Company or meeting of the holders of the Relevant Share Capital (as defined in sub-clause F of this Clause 4) or of any class thereof, nor the right to demand or vote on a poll which would have, but for this provision, attached to such shares. If after the close of such Offer for Sale none of the said shares is sold by NIBJ pursuant thereto, the above restrictions shall cease to apply until there is a subsequent sale of the said shares, or any of them, by NIBJ or Government as the case may be in which event the restrictions shall apply in relation to any of the said shares retained by NIBJ or Government after such sale.

K. Each director shall be indemnified out of the funds of the Company in respect of all costs, charges, losses, damages, suits and expenses which he shall incur or become liable to pay or which may be brought against him on account of any act, matter or thing which shall be done or undertaken by him in good faith and without neglect, default, breach of duty, or breach of trust on his part in relation to the Company in pursuance of any duty or function under Clause 4 thereof.

L. The amendment, or removal, or suspension, or alteration of the effect of any of the provisions of this Clause 4 shall not be effected unless by the authority of a resolution unanimously passed on a poll at an extraordinary general meeting of the Company, at which there are present, in person or by proxy, members together holding 90% of the voting rights in the Relevant Share Capital as defined in sub-clause F of this Clause.

APPENDIX 4

The British Gas Regulatory Formula in Detail

Condition 3: 'Restriction of Gas Prices to Tariff Customers' and Condition 4: 'Standing Charges', attached to the authorisation granted by the Secretary of State for Energy to the British Gas Corporation to supply gas under the Gas Act 1986:

Restriction of gas prices to tariff customers

1. The Supplier shall:
    (a) exercise its power to fix tariffs under section 14 of the Act so that no increase in the tariffs last fixed by the Supplier under section 25(3) of the 1972 Act has effect before 1st April 1987; and
    (b) in setting its prices for tariff customers having effect on or after 1st April 1987 take all reasonable steps, having particular regard to the interests of those customers, to secure that in each Relevant Year its Average Price per therm shall not exceed the Maximum Average Price per therm calculated in accordance with the following formula:

$$M_t = \left(1 + \frac{RPI_t - 2}{100}\right) \times P_{t-1} + Y_t - K_t$$

where

M_t = Maximum Average Price per therm in Relevant Year t;

RPI_t = the percentage change (whether of a positive or negative value) in the Retail Price Index between that published or determined with respect to October in Relevant Year t and that published or determined with respect to the immediately preceding October;

$$P_{t-1} = P_{t-2}\left(1 + \frac{\text{RPI}_{t-1} - 2}{100}\right)$$

but, in relation to the first Relevant Year, P_{t-1} (and, accordingly, in relation to the second Relevant Year, P_{t-2}) shall have a value equal to the Average Price per therm in the financial year commencing on 1st April 1986 less the Allowable Gas Cost per therm in that year all calculated as if the financial year commencing on 1st April 1986 were a Relevant Year;

Y_t = Allowable Gas Cost per therm in Relevant Year t;

K_t = the correction per therm (whether of a positive or negative value) to be made in Relevant Year t (other than the first Relevant Year) which is derived from the following formula:

$$K_t = \frac{T_{t-1} - (Q_{t-1}M_{t-1})}{Q_t}\left(1 + \frac{I_t}{100}\right)$$

in which

T_{t-1} = Tariff Revenue from Tariff Quantity in Relevant Year $t-1$;

Q_{t-1} = Tariff Quantity in Relevant Year $t-1$;

Q_t = Tariff Quantity in Relevant Year t;

M_{t-1} = Maximum Average Price per therm in Relevant Year $t-1$;

131

I_t = the percentage interest rate in Relevant Year t which is equal to, where K_t (taking no account of I_t for this purpose) has a positive value, the average Specified Rate plus three or, where K_t (taking no account of I_t for this purpose) has a negative value, the average Specified Rate.

The subscript t represents the Relevant Year.

2. In this Condition:

'Allowable Gas Cost' means the aggregate of the following amounts namely:

(a) the amounts paid or payable by the Supplier at any time to each vendor of gas (not being an associated company);

    (i) for, and wholly and exclusively related to, the quantity of gas delivered to the Supplier in the Relevant Year for the Supplier's Gas Supply Business (being payments of purchase price in pounds sterling, or, if not in pounds sterling, converted to pounds sterling at the spot rate of exchange in London for purchasing the relevant foreign currency as quoted by Barclays Bank plc at the close of business on the date of payment thereof); or

    (ii) as Capacity Charges in respect of the Relevant Year, but excluding any payments of interest and of any other amount payable by the Supplier because of any failure by the Supplier to perform its obligations or make any payment to vendors under its contract to purchase the gas so delivered; and deducting, where payment for gas is due more than 30 days after the end of the month of its delivery, a sum equal to the interest on the price of the gas for the period from 30 days after the end of the month of delivery to the date of payment, at the Specified Rate.

(b) (i) where, under the terms of a contract with a vendor of gas (not being an associated company), the Supplier has made a payment ('initial payment') with respect to gas not taken by it before the Relevant Year and, in that Relevant Year, the Supplier either takes gas by reason, wholly or partly, of that initial payment or, having taken gas in that Relevant Year for which

132

consideration has been paid or would otherwise be payable, is allowed a credit by reason, wholly or partly, of that initial payment (provided that the consideration which has been paid, or which would otherwise be payable, has not been included under paragraph 2)a) above–

(A) the amount of that initial payment to which the gas so taken is attributable; and

(B) an amount representing interest on that payment compounded annually from the date of payment calculated at the Specified Rate for the period beginning with that date and ending on the last day of the month in which the gas is taken or, as the case may be, the credit is allowed (and for this purpose payments and gas taken by reference to them shall be treated on a first in/first out basis);

(ii) where any initial payment has been made by the Supplier and, in the Relevant Year, either the terms of the contract have the effect, or it is shown to the reasonable satisfaction of the Director, that any gas will not be available for delivery, or credit which might otherwise have been allowed to the Supplier by reason wholly or partly of that payment will no longer be allowed, such amount over such period as the Director, after consultation with the Supplier, shall determine is a fair amount to be included in respect of any one or more Relevant Years;

(c) where any gas which is delivered to the Supplier is purchased by it for a consideration which is not wholly pecuniary or where gas and anything other than gas are purchased as part of the same transaction or arrangement by the Supplier, the amount which the Supplier demonstrates to the reasonable satisfaction of the Director would be the pecuniary consideration for the gas if negotiated at arm's length as between a willing vendor and a willing purchaser;

(d) where gas is purchased otherwise than at the Point of Delivery, such amount as is demonstrated to the reasonable satisfaction of the Director is or would be payable by the Supplier under a third party contract negotiated at arm's length for transporting the gas to the Point of Delivery and for any processing or treatment of the gas which is necessary to render it of suitable quality for entry into the Supplier's Transmission System;

(e) such amount as reflects the application of the following provisions, that is to say:

(i) where the Supplier in a Relevant Year appropriates to the Gas Supply Business gas which it produced itself or which it acquired from an associated company ('Own Gas'), the Supplier shall furnish to the Director as soon as practicable after the end of that year a written statement of the amount which the Supplier shall certify to the best of its information, knowledge and belief represents no more than the market value (as defined in the Oil Taxation Act 1975) of such gas, together with an explanation of how any such amount has been arrived at and the amount so certified may be included as an Allowable Gas Cost on an interim basis provided it is not greater than the amount with respect thereto included or to be included (either on a provisional or final basis) by the Supplier or associated company in its return to the Oil Taxation Office of the Inland Revenue (or such other department of the Inland Revenue as is appropriate) but if it is greater, the lower amount shall be included;

(ii) in the event of it being ascertained by the Oil Taxation Office of the Inland Revenue in agreement with the Supplier, or determined in legal proceedings, that the market value of any Own Gas for the purposes of the Oil Taxation Act 1975 (or, in the case of Own Gas the subject of a tax exempt contract, as defined in section 1(3) of the Gas Levy Act 1981, by any department of the Inland Revenue in agreement with the Supplier, or in legal proceedings, that the market value of any Own Gas for any other tax purposes) is different from the amount permitted by sub-paragraph (i) above to be included on an interim

134

basis for the purposes of the Allowable Gas Cost, the difference shall be reflected in an appropriate manner in the Allowable Gas Cost for the purposes of the formula described in paragraph 1 above and reported by the Supplier to the Director promptly after it has been ascertained or determined;

(f) an amount equal to the gas levy payable to the Secretary of State by the Supplier under the Gas Levy Act 1981 in respect of the aggregate quantity of gas of which account is to be taken for the purposes of calculating the amounts referred to in sub-paragraphs (a), (b), (c) and (e) above;

(g) any amount (whether or not similar to or different from expenditure of the kinds or amounts previously mentioned) which, after written application by and consultation with the Supplier, is determined by the Director to be a cost of gas acquired by the Supplier for the Supplier's Gas Supply Business or to be a cost otherwise fairly related to the gas acquired,

but no amount shall be a component of Allowable Gas Cost both under sub-paragraph (g) above and any other of the preceding sub-paragraphs or under more than one of those sub-paragraphs and for the purposes of this definition of 'Allowable Gas Cost', the delivery of gas shall be treated as taking place at the Point of Delivery.

For the purposes of any calculation which is made with respect to the financial year commencing on 1st April 1986, any amount which could reasonably qualify for inclusion in Allowable Gas Cost for that year under any of the preceding sub-paragraphs shall be so included notwithstanding the absence of any determination by or demonstration to the Director which would otherwise be required.

'Allowable Gas Cost per therm' means the Allowable Gas Cost in the Relevant Year divided by the Relevant Quantity in the Relevant Year.

'Average Price per therm' means Tariff Revenue in the Relevant Year divided by the Tariff Quantity of gas supplied in that Relevant Year.

'Capacity Charges' means any amounts which are of a recurring nature and are paid or payable by the Supplier in respect of the Relevant Year to a vendor of gas in order to reserve the availability to the Supplier of deliveries of gas in the year to which the amounts relate but not being any amounts which would fall to be treated in whole or in part as an advance payment (directly or indirectly) for gas.

'Point of Delivery' means the point at which gas, whether acquired by the Supplier from another person or produced or manufactured by it is, after such treatment as may be necessary to render it of suitable quality for entry into the Transmission System, first metered by the Supplier upon entry into the Transmission System.

'Relevant Quantity' means the aggregate of the following namely—

(a) the quantity of gas in therms delivered to the Supplier in the Relevant Year and purchased by it (otherwise than from an associated company) for the Supplier's Gas Supply Business being calculated where the price of gas is fixed by reference to an agreed calorific value, using that value, but if the agreed calorific value used in determining the price of the gas differs from the calorific value as measured, the Supplier shall give written notification to the Director of the amount of the difference;

(b) the quantity of Own Gas in therms appropriated by the Supplier in the Relevant Year to the Supplier's Gas Supply Business other than gas from the Rough reservoir.

'Specified Rate' means the base rate of Barclays Bank plc current from time to time during the period in respect of which the calculation falls to be made.

'Tariff Quantity' means the aggregate quantity of gas, in therms, supplied by the Supplier to tariff customers in the Relevant Year and taken into account for the purposes of determining Tariff Revenue.

'Tariff Revenue' means the turnover (measured on an accruals basis and including standing charges) derived from the supply of gas in the Relevant Year to tariff customers falling within the ordinary activities of the Gas Supply Business, after deduction of value added tax (if any) and any other taxes based directly on the amounts so derived.

3. (1) If in respect of any Relevant Year the Average Price per therm exceeds the Maximum Average Price per therm by more than 4 per cent of the latter, the Supplier shall furnish an explanation to the Director and in the next following Relevant Year the Supplier shall not effect any increase in prices unless it has demonstrated to the reasonable satisfaction of the Director that the Average Price per therm would not be likely to exceed the Maximum Average Price per therm in that next following Relevant Year;

(2) if, in respect of any two successive Relevant Years, the sum of the amounts by which the Average Price per therm has exceeded the Maximum Average Price per therm is more than 5 per cent of the Maximum Average Price per therm for the second of those years, then in the next following Relevant Year the Supplier shall, if required by the Director, adjust its prices such that the Average Price per therm would not be likely, in the judgement of the Director, to exceed the Maximum Average Price per therm in that next following Relevant Year;

(3) if in respect of each of two successive Relevant Years the Average Price per therm is less than 90 per cent of the Maximum Average Price per therm, the Director, after consultation with the Supplier, may direct that, in calculating K_t in respect of the next following Relevant Year, there shall be substituted for T_{t-1} in the formula set out in paragraph 1 above such figure as the Director may specify being not less than T_{t-1} and not more than $0.90(Q_{t-1}M_{t-1})$.

4. (1) Where the Supplier publishes any change in the price of gas (which shall include any change in standing charges) which it proposes to make to tariff customers, the Supplier shall not later than the time of such publication provide the Director with—

(a) a written forecast of the Maximum Average Price per therm, together with its components, in respect of the Relevant Year in which the change of price of gas is to take effect and also in respect of the next following Relevant Year; and

(b) a written estimate of the Maximum Average Price per therm, together with its components, in respect of the Relevant Year immediately preceding the Relevant Year in which the change in price of gas is to take effect unless a statement complying with paragraph 4(5) below in respect of that first mentioned Relevant Year has been furnished to the Director before the publication of the proposed change in gas price;

(2) if within three months of the commencement of any Relevant Year the Supplier has not published or effected any change in price as is referred in sub-paragraph (1) above the Supplier shall provide the Director with a written forecast of the Maximum Average Price per therm, together with its components, in respect of that Relevant Year;

(3) any forecasts as aforesaid shall be accompanied by such information as regards the assumptions (such as economic growth, exchange rate changes and energy prices) which are critical features thereof as may be necessary to enable the Director to be reasonably satisfied that the forecasts have been properly prepared on a consistent basis;

(4) not later than 6 weeks after the end of a Relevant Year the Supplier shall send to the Director a statement as to whether or not in its opinion paragraph 3(1), (2) or (3) applies in respect of that Relevant Year and its best estimate of what K is likely to be in the following Relevant Year;

(5) not later than 3 months after the end of a Relevant Year the Supplier shall send to the Director a statement, in respect of that Relevant Year, and for the purposes of this sub-paragraph and sub-paragraphs (6) and (7) below the financial year commencing on 1st April 1986 shall be treated as a Relevant Year, showing–

(a) Allowable Gas Cost;

(b) Relevant Quantity;

(c) Tariff Revenue;

(d) Tariff Quantity;

(6) the statement referred to in sub-paragraph (5) above shall be–

(a) accompanied by a report from the Auditor that in his opinion such statement fairly presents Allowable Gas Cost, Relevant Quantity, Tariff Revenue and Tariff Quantity in accordance with the requirements of this Condition and that the amount of Tariff Revenue and, so far as applicable, the amount included as Allowable Gas Cost are in accordance with the Supplier's accounting records which have been maintained in accordance with Condition 2; and

(b) certified by a person appointed under section 1(2) of the 1972 Act, or if this Authorisation has effect as if granted to the successor company, by a director of the Supplier, that no amount included within Allowable Gas Cost represents other than bona fide consideration for gas delivered for use in the Gas Supply Business or an amount permitted under this Condition to be so included;

provided that where any component of Allowable Gas Cost requires to be determined by, or demonstrated to the satisfaction of, the Director or is subject, under paragraph 2(e)(ii) of this Condition, to adjustment, and the determination, demonstration or adjustment has not been made by the date when the statement under this paragraph is sent to the Director, that statement and the report and certificate in respect of it may be qualified accordingly;

(7) for the avoidance of doubt and without prejudice to the obligations of the Supplier under this Condition, it is recognised that where, after any Relevant Year, it is shown that any amount which has been or has not been included in the amount of the Allowable Gas cost for that year should not have been or should have been included (as the case may be) in the Allowable Gas Cost for that year, the 'Maximum Average Price' shall be recalculated on the basis of the actual amounts for each Relevant Year up to and including the Relevant Year in which the

inclusion or non-inclusion of the amount was so shown.

5. (1) This condition shall apply so long as this Authorisation continues in force but shall cease to have effect if–

    (a) the Supplier delivers to the Director a written request ('disapplication request') made in accordance with sub-paragraph (2) below and the Director agrees in writing to the disapplication request; or

    (b) its application is terminated by notice given by the Supplier in accordance with either sub-paragraph (3) or sub-paragraph (4) below;

  (2) any disapplication request shall be in writing, addressed to the Director, and shall state the date ('disapplication date') from which the Supplier wishes the Director to agree that this Condition shall cease to have effect, but the disapplication date therein stated shall not be before whichever is the later of 1st April 1992 and any date which is less than 18 months after the date upon which the disapplication request is delivered to the Director;

  (3) if the Director has not made a reference to the Monopolies Commission under section 24 of the Act relating to the modification of this Condition before the beginning of the period of 12 months which will end with the disapplication date, the Supplier may deliver written notice to the Director terminating the application of this Condition with effect from the disapplication date or a later date;

  (4) if the Monopolies Commission makes a report on a reference made by the Director relating to the modification of this Condition after a disapplication request and such report does not include a conclusion that the cessation of this Condition, in whole or in part, operates, or may be expected to operate, against the public interest, the Supplier may within 30 days after the publication of the report by the Director deliver to him written notice terminating the application of the Condition with effect from the disapplication date or a later date.

Condition 4: Standing Charges

1. The Supplier shall secure that on and after 1st April 1987 any standing charges payable by tariff customers in any Relevant Year do not exceed the standing charges payable by such customers under the tariffs last fixed by the Supplier under section 25(3) of the 1972 Act increased by the percentage increase in the amount of the Retail Price Index published or determined for the month of December immediately preceding that Relevant Year over the amount of the Retail Price Index published for the month of December 1985.

2. This Condition shall apply *mutatis mutandis* to any change in or imposition of charges having a similar effect on a tariff customer to a standing charge.

3. This Condition shall cease to have effect if Condition 3 ceases to have effect by virtue of paragraph 5 of that Condition.

APPENDIX 5

*Summary of Contents of Accountant's Long-Form
Report of the Kind Used in UK Privatisations*

1. HISTORY AND DEVELOPMENT OF BUSINESS
   (a) History and recent development of business
   (b) Corporate legal structure
   (c) Present capital structure
   (d) Recent legislation
   (e) Research for future
2. OPERATIONS
   A detailed description of operations analysed by segments
   including:
   (a) Activities/services provided
   (b) Staff utilisation
   (c) Processes involved
   (d) Facilities and their utilisation
   (e) Customers and terms of trade
   (f) Research and development facilities
3. MANAGEMENT AND EMPLOYEES
   (a) Management structure and organisation:
     – The Corporation
     – Headquarters
     – Executive roles and divisional structure
     – Production and supply
     – Marketing
     – Resources and external affairs
     – Finance
     – Economic planning
     – Personnel
     – Research and development
     – Secretariat
     – Legal

- Headquarters committee structure
- Committees reporting to the Corporation
- Committees reporting to the Executive
- National policy and advisory committees
- Panels
- Regions
- Regional management structure
- Regional committee structure
- Exploration companies

(b) Key Personnel:
- Pen portraits of Directors
- Emoluments of Directors
- Earnings of the top employees
- Other key employees
- Management development and succession procedures
- Comparative remuneration data

(c) Service Contracts

(d) Staff and Employees:
- Summarised statistics of employee categories
- Grading schemes
- Promotion structure
- Education and training
- Overview of pay structure
- Comparative remuneration data
- Terms and conditions of employment
- Car schemes and other employee benefits
- Manpower planning
- External recruitment
- Equal opportunities

(e) Industrial Relations:
- Employee representative bodies
- Summary of trade union membership requirements and statistics
- Recent industrial relations issues and lost time disputes

(f) Pension Arrangements:
- Salient features of the pension schemes
- Administration of the pension schemes
- Investment strategy

143

- – Summary of pension scheme accounts
- – Actuarial valuations
4. OVERALL ASSESSMENT OF SYSTEMS
   (a) Financial records and accounting systems
   (b) Costing systems
   (c) Management information systems
5. FINANCIAL
   (a) Accounting policies
      - – statement of accounting policies and details of changes in the last five years together with details of actual adjustments made in the period under review
      - – details of variations of accounting policy from normal accounting principles and standards
      - – details of variations of accounting policy from normal industry practices
      - – analysis and suggestions on alternate bases and accounting principles on all material matters such as research and development, depreciation, construction work in progress, capitalised interest, exploration expenditure, off-balance sheet financing, valuation of stocks, taxation, pension commitments, exchange fluctuations, movements in reserves, valuation of assets
   (b) Statement of adjustments
   (c) Accounts reconciliation:
      - – detailed reconciliation between historic cost results, current cost accounts and published figures
   (d) Trading results (P&L) for last five years by each activity and consolidated results including:
      - – results prepared under historic cost and current cost conventions
      - – analysis of turnover, expenses and profitability of business activity
      - – analysis of expenses of following
         (i) essential services
         (ii) research and development
         (iii) head office and other administrative expenses
      - – analysis and details of the bases and principles of cost allocation and transfer pricing
      - – analysis of trends disclosed by above investigation. In

144

particular, the analysis of movements in turnover, expenses, and profitability between volume increases, price increases, purchase and other cost increases, exchange fluctuations, operational changes and changes in accounting policies

(e) Taxation including:
- review of taxation changes and taxation liabilities for the last five years
- status of corporation tax computations
- discussion of other taxes and status
- other significant tax matters

(f) Balance Sheet including:
- analytical review and commentary on historic and current costs balance sheets for last five years by each of the main categories of assets and liabilities

(g) Cash-flow statement (last five years)

(h) Borrowings
- current position
- facilities and utilisation
- off-balance sheet financing
- guarantees
- terms – i.e. period, amount, rate, repayment schedule
- security
- covenants
- restrictions

(i) Other matters including:
- insurance and litigation
- performance measured against government and company targets
- contingencies
- material contracts
- capital commitments

6. CORPORATE PLAN AND FORECASTING

(a) Assessment of the systems:
- Strategic and medium-term planning
- Budgeting
- Budgetary control and forecasting

(b) Review of actual results against budget:
- Turnover variances

- Cost variances
- Current cost and adjustments
- Interest variances
- Taxation variances

(c) Assumptions and sensitivity:
- Assumptions
- Sensitivity

(d) Forecasts during the year

(e) Budgeting for cash and funds flow:
- Treasury management
- Capital expenditure

7. PROFIT FORECAST

(a) Profit forecast for current financial year including:
- Summarised P&L accounts
- Proforma P&L accounts
- Summary of sales forecasts
- Summary of trading costs
- Segmental analysis of operating profit
- Sensitivity of profit forecast

(b) Working capital forecast including:
- fund-flow statement
- cash-flow statement

(c) Review of unaudited accounts:
- summarised P&L
- summarised balance sheet

(d) Comparison of actual results with budgets

(e) Strategic and medium-term planning, budgeting and forecasting

(f) List of principal assumptions

BIBLIOGRAPHY

Much of the material contained in this book is derived from practical experience and confidential files, from which non-confidential information has been extracted. Listed below are the publicly available sources from which additional material has been drawn.

Books and Pamphlets

Adam Smith Institute, *Impact of Ideas* (n.d.)

Adam Smith Institute, *Privatisation Worldwide* (n.d.)

AIMS for Industry, *Report of Public Opinion of Labour's Nationalisation Policy* (n.d.)

Audit Commission Occasional Paper, *Competitiveness and Contracting-out of Local Authorities Services* (February 1987)

Bassett, P., *Strike Free* (Macmillan, London, 1986)

Beckermann, W., ed., *The Labour Government's Economic Record 1964–1970* (Duckworth, London, 1979)

Beresford, P., *Good Council Guide, Wandsworth 1978–1987* (Centre for Policy Studies, London, 1987)

Blackstone Franks, Chartered Accountants, *The Economist Guide to Management Buy-Outs 1986–1987* (Economist Publications, London, 1987)

Boyson, R., ed., *Goodbye to Nationalisation* (Churchill Press, London, 1971)

Bradley, K. and Gelb, A., *Share Ownership for Employees* (Public Policy Centre, London, 1986)

Butler, D. and Butler, G., *British Political Facts 1900–1986* (Macmillan, London, 1987)

Centre for Policy Studies, *Why Britain Needs a Social Market Economy* (London, 1975)

Cottrel, E., *Steel: The Giant with the Feet of Clay – The British Steel Industry 1945–1981* (Centre for Policy Studies, London, 1981)

Crosland, C.A.R., *The Future of Socialism* (Jonathan Cape, London, 1963)

de Croisset, C., Prot, B. and de Rosen, M., *Dénationalisation, Les Leçons de l'Etranger* (Economica, Paris, 1987)

Eatwell, R., *The 1945–1951 Labour Governments* (Batsford Academic Press, London, 1979)

Energy Act 1983 (HMSO, London)

Forsyth, M., *Barriers to Privatisation* (AIMS, n.d.)

Haitari, K., *The Japanese Economic System* (Heath, Lexington, MA, 1986)

Hatch, J. and Redwood, J., *Controlling Public Industries* (Blackwell, Oxford, 1982)

Home Affairs Committee Report, *Contract Provisions of Prisons* (HMSO, London, 25 March 1987)

Hough, J.R., *The French Economy* (Croom Helm, London, 1982)

Institute of Directors Policy Unit, *The Political Environment for Business* (London, December 1985)

Katzenstein, P., *Corporatism and Change: Austria, Switzerland and the Politics of Industry* (Cornell University Press, London, 1984)

Kay, J., Mayer, C. and Thompson, D., *Privatisation and Regulation: The UK Experience* (Oxford University Press, Oxford, 1986)

Kelf-Cohen, R., *Twenty Years of Nationalisation* (Macmillan, London, 1969)

Loyrette, J., 'Remarques sur le problème des dénationalisations' (Paris, May 1985)

Marlin, J.T., Editor in chief, *Privatisation of Local Government Activities – Lessons from Japan* (The National Civics league, New York, 1982)

Mathias, P., *The First Industrial Nation* (Methuen, London, 1969)

McLachlan, S., *The National Freight Buy-Out* (Macmillan, London, 1983)

Minford, P., Savas, E.S. and Mays, I., *Privatisation in Practice* (Selsdon Group, Viewpoint Series)

Moore, J., *Privatisation in the United Kingdom* (AIMS, London, n.d.)

Moore, R., *Emergence of the Labour Party 1880–1964* (Hodder and Stoughton, London, 1978)

OFTEL, *Public Telecommunications Operators Contract Terms and*

Conditions – A Contract Document (London, August 1987)

Ohashi, T.M. and Roth, T.P., *Privatisation: Theory and Practice* (Fraser Institute, Vancouver, 1980)

Parris, H., Pestieau, P. and Saynor, P., *Public Enterprise in Western Europe* (Croom Helm, London, 1987)

Pirie, M., *Privatisation in Theory and in Practice* (Adam Smith Institute, London, 1985)

Pollard, S., *Development of the British Economy 1914–1967* (Edward Arnold, London, 1973)

Price Waterhouse, *Budget Memorandum* (London, 1987)

Price Waterhouse, *Privatisation: The Facts* (London, July, 1987)

Redwood, J., *Public Enterprise in Crisis* (Blackwell, Oxford, 1980)

Robert, R., *Chartered Companies* (G. Bell & Sons Ltd., London, 1969)

Sanhai, J.-J., Broclawski, J.-P., Longueville, G. and Ohel, P., *Les Privatisations a l'Etranger* (Les Documentations Français, Paris, 1986)

Sherman, Sir Alfred, *The Crisis Calls for a Minister for Denationalisation* (AIMS, London, undated)

Stock Exchange, *Survey of Share Ownership* (London, 1987)

Stock Exchange, *What is the History of the Stock Exchange?* (London, 1987)

Telecommunications Act 1984 (HMSO, London)

HM Treasury, *Privatisation in the United Kingdom – Background Briefing*

Tupper, A. and Dean, G.B., eds, *Public Corporations and Public Policy in Canada* (Institute for Research on Public Policy, 1981)

Veljanovski, C., *Selling the State* (Weidenfeld & Nicolson, London, 1981)

Webb, R.K., *Modern England* (George Allen & Unwin, London, 1969)

Speeches, Articles and Party Political Documents

Channon, P., Speech to Bow Group (8 December 1986)

Chataway, C., *New Deal for Industry* (Conservative Political Centre, London, 1972)

Conservative Party *Campaign Guides*, 1951–1987

Conservative Party Manifestos, 1964–1987

Conservative Programme 1970, *A Better Tomorrow*

Conservative Programme 1976, *The Right Approach*

Conservative Programme 1977, *The Right Approach to the Economy*

Cox, W., 'Privatisation in the Public Services', paper delivered at the Fraser Institute Conference on Privatisation (Vancouver, 24 July 1987)

Davies, David G., 'The Efficiency of Public versus Private Firms: The Case of Australia's Two Airlines', *Journal of Law and Economics*, vol. 14, April 1971

Davies, David G., 'The Australian Airlines Revisited', *Journal of Law and Economics*, vol. 20, April 1977

Fortier, P., *Privatisation of Crown Properties* (Quebec, February, 1986)

Henderson, D., *Innocence and Design*, 1985 Reith Lectures

Joseph, Sir Keith, *Inflation Retards Growth* (London, 1974)

Labour Party Conference Reports 1981–1986

Labour Party Manifestos 1964–1987

Labour's Programme 1972, 1973, 1976

McDavid, J., 'Privatisation in Local Governments in Canada', paper delivered at the Fraser Institute Conference on Privatisation (Vancouver, 24 July 1987)

Moore, J., 'Results of Privatisation', paper presented to Financial Times Conference (16 November 1983)

Moore, J., 'The Success of Privatisation' (speech, 17 July 1985)

Moore, J., *The Value of Ownership* (Conservative Political Centre, London, 1986)

Moore, J., *Why Privatise?* (Conservative Political Centre, London, 1983)

Mount, F., *The Practice of Liberty* (Conservative Political Centre, London, 1986)

Schwartz, D.R., 'Privatisation of State and Local Government Services in the USA', paper presented at the Fraser Institute Conference on Privatisation (24 July 1987)

Trades Union Congress Conference Reports, 1981–6

HM Treasury Economic Progress Report, *Wider Share Ownership*

Company Documents

SHARE OFFER PROSPECTUSES

Amersham International

Associated British Ports
British Aerospace
British Airports Authority
British Airways
British Gas
British Gas (American Depositary Shares)
British Gas (European Prospectus)
British Petroleum I
British Telecom
Britoil I
Britoil II
Cable and Wireless
Caribbean Cement Company
Conrail
Enterprise Oil
Jaguar
National Commercial Bank Ltd
Paribas (International Prospectus)
Petrocorp
Rhône–Poulenc SA (American Depositary Shares)
Rolls-Royce
Saint Gobain
Société Générale (International Prospectus)
TSB

OTHERS
British Gas Securities Registration Statement
IRI Yearbooks 1985, 1986
National Commercial Bank Ltd, Memorandum and Articles
National Freight Corporation Annual Reports 1984–6
Vickers Annual Reports 1984–6

Newspapers and Journals

Various articles were used from the following:
Australian Financial Review
Birmingham Post
British Business
Christian Science Monitor

The Daily Gleaner (Kingston, Jamaica)
The Daily Telegraph
Dow Jones News Retrieval Service
East Anglian Daily Times
The Economist
Euromoney Corporate Finance
Evening Standard
Far Eastern Economic Review
The Financial Times
The Financial Times Supplements
Glasgow Herald
Global Analysis Systems
The Guardian
Investor
JIJI Press
Libération
Lloyds Bank Review
Lloyds' List
Le Monde
El País
The Observer
The Scotsman
The Sunday Telegraph
The Sunday Times
The Times
Toronto Globe and Mail
Yorkshire Post

INDEX

Note. Only major firms are included, others being subsumed under industry type e.g. electricity. The origin of non-British firms is indicated in brackets where necessary.

153